15.95

THE WARRIOR

TALES OF A SUBSTITUTE TEACHER AND JOB COACH

A MEMOIR

ANDY PALASCIANO

LYMER & HART

GARDEN OAK PRESS

Rainbow, California

gardenoakpress.com

Lymer & Hart
Garden Oak Press
1953 Huffstatler St., Suite A
Rainbow, CA 92028
760 728-2088
gardenoakpress.com
gardenoakpress@gmail.com

First published on February 15, 2019
        by Lymer & Hart / Garden Oak Press

ISBN-13: 978-1-7323753-1-4
ISBN-10: 1-7323753-1-3

Lymer & Hart is an imprint of Garden Oak Press

Printed in the United States of America

What if *The Hokey Pokey*
    really is what it's all about?
                    — Anonymous

Before the Beginning

I have always had an ability to get lost.
You know how kids look up and the shopping cart they are holding onto is not their mom's? That was me. Every time.

One time I went through a series of women's dressing rooms looking for my mom. I opened each curtain and said, "Mom?"

I still remember those screaming women.

My mom has a similar ability.

Driving me around when I was a kid, she'd smile: "If we hadn't gotten lost we never would have seen this."

We saw a lot, and, in the same way, in my life I have, too.

But through my working career, I began to find my way. This book is a road map of that journey.

THE WARRIOR

TALES OF A SUBSTITUTE TEACHER AND JOB COACH

a memoir

ANDY PALASCIANO

My employment career started out slow.

I worked as a dishwasher and as a warehouse register boy (where I got demoted to conveyer belt boy). I worked as a metal shop laborer and was let go in a week.

I worked as a vacuum salesman for two weeks. Here I got to say: "Hey, youngster, you see this marble? I'm going to make it disappear. And, look! Out it comes inside the vacuum. How much would you pay for this little beauty, because I've got a surprise for you. No, stop guessing! This vacuum *can be yours* for a mere $2000!"

My natural ability to get lost didn't help. I had a carpet cleaning job where I averaged about 25 U-turns a day. And, of course, I always took jobs like those. I had a food delivery job and set the record for the longest delivery – over three hours. I remember telling my boss on the intercom:

"Listen, that address is not here! O – K!?"

I even had a messenger job once. That one probably doesn't require me to go into detail.

But the job that best demonstrated my talents came just before I became a Substitute Teacher: copier of legal documents.

Basically, I had a giant camera that I would feed a document into. No copy was made there – only a picture was taken and the document came out the other side of the camera. After work, I delivered the film to my boss. This helped me improve my U-turn average. I was on a roll.

After a month, my boss told me, "You know that lady from the downtown facility you copy from? She indicated that it might be best if you never come around again. Sorry, Andy. I'm going to have to let you go. Not one of the copies you made in the past month has come out."

A week later, my boss was fired and a couple of weeks after that, the office went out of business.

Guess they couldn't make it without me.

And it's not like I'm a natural with children either.

There was this one time when I was visiting my brother who lives in the woods. I took my two nieces, ages one and five, to see the horse in the backyard. As the only adult, I was the one who grabbed the electric fence.

Equipped with these experiences, plus a questionable college degree and absolutely no teacher training – and having passed a third-grade math test – I was finally ready to teach.

I became a Substitute Teacher right out of college. I had a lot of pride in my life. It was about to be cleansed of that pride through chalkboard dust and paper wads.

I was a different person then, one who trusted only in himself. If I had to live it again, I would be scared to follow myself, the jolly thinker at the wheel. Thankfully I don't have to live it again. But now I can look back and laugh.

The first class I ever taught was high school math.

I got there late and found no lesson plans. So I learned, I think from a student, that I was supposed to go over the previous night's homework. I looked at the work and had no idea how to do it.

Convinced I had to maintain authoritative control over the class, I stared at them stone-faced, fearing I'd be exposed as a fraud.

"You, in the front row," I told a student. "Come up and do the problem on the board. And class, you tell him if he's right or wrong. I'm not going to help you. You guys should know how to do this stuff."

It worked.

I got another assignment similar to that one. Waking up late, I threw on pants my mom had just bought me and I drove to class. Still trying to maintain authoritative poise in this high school math class, I spotted a girl raising her hand and snapped at her, "What?"

"Do you know you have the tag from the store on those pants?"

I quieted the class, but 10 minutes later, that same girl raised her hand: "Do you know you have another tag on those pants?"

I'm more careful with my attire these days.

T eaching another class – high school French? – two students came up to my desk and asked me if they could get a drink. "Ok," I told them, amazed at how well I was handling this class. The students came back, their arms full of soda, and started calling out, "Who had the 7-Up? And Dr. Pepper?" and began distributing the cans around the class.

I think I got a Diet Coke.

P owerless permanent teachers bowed down to tyrannical Substitutes. Substitute Teachers wielded the real power. A Substitute is like a Chihuahua that jumps when it barks: *Arf arf arf.* And people bow down and pay their respect. This raw power helped me see where I was going more clearly, even if the glare from the dog tag on my collar was a little bright.

Substitute Power

T here was a teacher's strike this week and the teachers called the real power brokers of their profession, the Substitute Teachers. The Substitutes, and the Substitutes alone, have the power to tell our government leaders it is time for change.

One Substitute Teacher easily gained control of the ear of the audience and said at the rally, "I spoke to Congressman William Gillespie today and said, `Bill, things need to change. I've got these permanent teachers complaining about this and that and I just can't have it. What are we going to do about this?'

"Congressman Gillespie then looked at me and said, `Anything for you, sir. We are going to change things right away.'

"And I said, 'I appreciate it, Bill. Sorry to come here in such a hurry. Say hi to Margerie.' And the Congressman drafted a bill that night. He brought it over to my house to see if I would approve it. I looked it over and said, 'No, I want my teachers making 10 percent more!'"

The crowd cheered.

The Substitute took the applause in stride and kept going:

"Bill said, 'Right away, no problem!' So teachers be patient. Be brave. Things will get easier."

The rally had a relaxed moment. One thing became clear: when a Substitute Teacher speaks, everyone listens.

OF THE FORTRESS
OF DURA

SUBFINDER

ubfinder is the computer system that notified Substitutes of a job. Sometimes I would get 80 *Subfinder* calls in one weekend. Some nights I would come home and my brother would say, "*Subfinder* mounted a fine attack last night, about 20 calls."

If I had been expecting a personal call, it would piss me off. And there's almost nothing I could do, especially since I was trying to get a job for the next day. Sometimes I would take a job that I knew I couldn't teach just to shut *Subfinder* up. I could scream, "Hah, *Subfinder*, your kingdom fades!"

I taught music classes where I ordered a kid to conduct the orchestra. I taught a drum class where kids beat drums with their hands and fingers. I taught fashion design. All the while I could hear *Subfinder* laughing at me.

It was always disheartening to be awakened at 5 a.m. by a *Subfinder* attack. I struggled to find the phone in the dark. Disoriented to any kind of reality, I would hear a computer voice:

"This is the *Subfinder* system. You will substitute for (a woman with a Spanish accent chimes in) "Maria Conchita Consuela Gonzalez."

I would always assume this was an English speaking class. The school was supposed to tell you if it's for Spanish-speaking students. But many schools don't reveal that, because they're afraid that they won't get a Sub.

Twice these Spanish *Subfinder* messages did yield an English speaking class. All the other times—many, many other times—I would be greeted with an "Hola!" as I walked into the classroom.

Spanish words on the walls. Spanish color pronunciation on the rug. Hanging my head, I could only say, "Yo no hablo Español."

A teacher's aide would then teach the class, while I sulked in the corner.

I had one Spanish-speaking Special Ed class where the aide left me alone for about half an hour while she went to lunch. I watched her say, "Bye," almost in slow motion. The minute she left, the kids jumped me. One took an arm, one took a leg, then my other arm and other leg. The secluded classroom was dark—it was supposed to be quiet time—so no one could see in. I didn't know any Spanish to make them stop. I yelled, "No más!" and "No es bueno!" but no one could hear me scream.

I n college, a friend and I went to Mexico for what we thought was Spring Break. It ended up being the Mexican Spring Break, not American Spring Break week.

We arrived in San Felipe without cash. The whole town had no ATMs and didn't accept credit cards. We ended up on the street. But God was working. We never missed a meal and some guys let us stay at their trailer on a lake a mile from the beach. They had jet skis and four-wheel ATVs. It was awesome.

I grew a lot that week. I still remember driving out of town, encountering a fire truck in the lane to the right of us, its sirens on. I knew I had to pull over, so I sped up, got in front of it and pulled over. I still remember my friend saying, "You cut off a fire truck to pull over?"

I wrote a poem about this. In it, I'm driving to an art show called *Cosmic Hollywood*. I see a fire truck with its sirens going and I say, "What would Cosmic Hollywood do?"

I pulled in front of the fire truck and swerved back and forth like a cop leading a sig alert. Then I took off my shirt and waved it out of the window, yelling, "Clear the road!"

The fireman yelled back at me. "You're driving an '85 Gremlin, waving your shirt out the window. And the yelling isn't helping!"

2

ZE DRUGS

When I became a Sub I was in my early twenties, I had just gotten out of college. I would "party" just like everyone else in college. I experimented with marijuana, but never liked it. Not only did it make me make say things, like "There are no rocks at the bottom of the ocean," but it made me paranoid.

This paranoia was mainly centered around people finding out the truth about me – that I was a blockhead.

I don't think I succeeded in hiding this anyway.

Though marijuana in my college days didn't cause my clouded cluelessness, it didn't help. It left me more lost than ever. I remember hearing someone of the older generation mistakenly referring to kids who smoke pot as "zoners" instead of stoners. I was a *zoner* then, to be sure, but not in that sense of the word. I had stopped smoking pot before my days of teaching. But sometimes going to work didn't help.

I got a call one morning for Clair Burgener Academy, thinking, "Oh, an academy, that should be easy." I drove there. It was a reform school.

One kid in my class asked, "Hey man, you smoke pot?"

I told him, "No."

Later in class I smelled something coming from the back of the room. This same kid was smoking pot. The more I thought about it, I more I figured that he hadn't want to be rude, so by asking me earlier, he had actually offered me to join him.

On another morning, I thought an elementary school would be safe.

I was wrong.

Reading a book to my second grade class, I began to believe the story was fixated on marijuana. In the house the clock was broken – permanently stopped on 4:20. The two characters, an old lady and her dog, leave the house and when they come back, the dog bounces, *Bong, bong, bong, bong, bong, bong,* into the house.

None of my students saw anything in this, but it was there. So I gave them all a stick of chewing gum and they peeled off the foil and pressed it all over their faces and arms.

"Did you know Big Red foil cleans your pores?" one of the students asked me.

This nonsense reminded me that as a teenager, I used to own a book that promised drugs would take me to amazing places in my mind. I wrote a poem about where marijuana had led me.

When sweet leaf
introduced me to my mind

I was excited to finally
be in my mind

Then I asked my ego,
"What do you want to do?"

And it said,
"I don't know what do you want to do?"

And I said,
"I don't know what do you want to do?"

And it said,
"I don't know."

Drugs led me absolutely nowhere.

As a kid, I remember a painting at a craft store – out front beneath the trees. It was a painting, yes, but it had three-dimensional live action scenes in it. The painting had depth, it had layers beneath the main surface, of a life at a mill—the main subject. I felt my life resembled that painting. It had depth of character. As a child, I felt like I was just as much the forest as I was a kid. But drugs at a young age made me live from the outside in.

Drugs made things so muddy, I couldn't see who I was or where I was going. I wanted to impress my friends and make them like me. But I was a fake. I didn't feel I could be liked or loved. I only felt vanity. I needed to love God and myself. This would become a daily challenge.

I had to realize I didn't owe the world anything. But there I sat, the moppet boy in the yellow chair.

As a teenager, I would sit in a yellow leather chair in my parents' house, thinking that because this was such a nice chair in such a nice house—fancier than our house in my home state—I could sit here and the world would live for me. But the world couldn't live for me, not for 50 million dollars or 50 billion-million (unless I used Visa, because, I remembered, *Life takes Visa*.)

That delusion was as ridiculous as a show my brother saw on a sports station: Rock-Paper-Scissors competition. And the pro players had characters like pro wrestlers:

"She's a cagey veteran who plays by her own rules."

"She's famous for using scissors!"

So, as a depressed teenager, I sat in his yellow leather chair in the dark, wasting away. I waited for the world to live for me. No one called me.

Even my mirror didn't work. I would stare at my reflection and resolve that I wasn't going to leave the bathroom until I had made a facial expression that convinced me I was now the best and that there would be no risk in my life from now on. That mirror failed me, too.

I could try other mirrors, and believe me I did. But drugs didn't help my predicament. Drugs made me crazy. I would write this wacked-out philosophy and speak to my friends in the words I wrote. If someone asked me how I was doing I might have said, "Undernourished gopherstacle and moonbeams, bro!"

I wrote a poem about this: *The Movie Version of Jim Morrison*.

Would you like a glass of grape juice, Jim?
We can always whip the horse's eyes.
What, Jim? What?
I love my girl.

B ack then, I might have told you the Milky Way was my idea. I might have said, "I saw this rag-tag group of planets and thought, You'd make one hell of a galaxy!"

Friends I made during that time meant well. They can be summed up best by my experience one night at a 7-11. I ordered a hot dog. The young guy behind the counter was so obviously stoned. He kept talking to his friend and laughing. I finally said, "Are you going to get my hot dog?"

"You ordered a hot dog? Trippy!"

I couldn't be there for my friends either in the state I was in, but I always thought I would be there for them, unlike the way they weren't there for me. I always had to call everyone else. They never called me. I wanted to be there for them, but couldn't. Only God could do that. I confused identities with God for a long time.

My older brother Dan would take me to the house where he lived, at the base of these foothills. As a kid, I remember thinking, *The hills are alive.* Those foothills were green at the time. Dan and his friends he lived with were like a breath of fresh air. God was showing me grace.

We would play Wiffle Ball in the back yard. His friend John, who always cracked me up, would fall to the ground on an inside pitch and act as if he was furious. It was almost too funny to watch.

Dan introduced me to music, and he and his friend made me tapes. They made me an old U2 and REM tape, but didn't list the songs by titles. Instead, they wrote a lyric from the songs. One of them was, "There's a comic strip that makes me laugh."

God was with me and blessing me even when I was in such a dark time. Did God like that I was lost? No, but He gave me grace to get through it.

My brother played the video game Tecmo Bowl, a football game. He chose the San Francisco 49ers, but rather than throw to Jerry Rice, a play that almost always works, Dan would run the fullback Rathman up the middle every time and get a first down each time.

A friend he was playing against finally shouted, "Who's your Offensive Coordinator?"

Even though I was lost, God's grace was all around me and He was with me, carrying me to a better place. My brothers and my sister were my Offensive Coordinators, there to guide me out of that dark place, as well as my parents. They guided me to see I was part of a bigger family, the family of God.

IMMEASURABLE

My name is on the board,"
"Can we call you Mister P?"
"Yeah, that's fine."
"Can we call you Master P?"
"Well, I don't like that as much, but. . . It's a funny story, I —"
A kid made a move toward the light switch. I have never had a positive result after someone flicked the lights on and off. It felt like slow motion. I said, "Nooooo."

Another kid made eye contact with the kid at the switch and said, "Turn it off. It's your destiny."

The kid walked away from the switch without turning the lights off.

Another time, a student was playing with blocks. I asked him what he was building. He said, "A hotel."

And this thing really looked like a hotel. Another kid moved one of the blocks and the hotel-building kid, dead serious, said, "Don't ! You'll upset the balance of nature."

I laughed. He looked up at me, still serious, now baffled. "What?"

This kid was a prodigy. The other day we were watching *Rudolph the Red Nosed Reindeer* and I was listening while working on something else. I noticed how completely random the movie was, yet it worked somehow. One minute the characters sang about silver and gold, and the next about a dentist elf, and then reindeer — one of them with a red nose — were flying.

After the movie this same kid said, "That was weird!"

Most kids got caught up in how magical the story was.

13

The kids taught me to love others and enjoy my life.

One girl saw me in the hall: "Mr. P!"

Another girl, who was not in my class, looked at me as if I was a mark. "This guy is a teacher? He's like one of us."

I felt honored to be on their level. On that level, the kids taught me to have fun and accept others. There were many students who individually taught me so much.

I was playing soccer with one kid, and he juked around me, saying, "That was called the circle of death."

Then he juked me again with a different move. And I asked, "What was that move?"

Calm and serious, he told me, "That was the triangle of mercy."

He went on matter-of-factly juking me, almost bored as he named each move. I've forgotten the names of most of his moves, but I remember him.

One day, after a storm, a rainbow appeared. One of the students gave me a trinket at the end of the school day and said, "Mr. P, can you put this at the end of the rainbow?"

I drove out of the parking lot and headed toward the end of the rainbow. I'm not sure if I reached the end of it. But I put the trinket in a field.

Dreams were being planted all the time.

3

WHERE WAS I?

"WHO ARE YOU SUBBING FOR?"
"HUH YEA, I DON'T KNOW"

The craziest thing about one school district was that six schools looked identical to each other. If the movie *Contact* has taught me anything, it's that "The oldest rule in government is why build one when you can build two at twice the price?" What if what was true in that movie was true in this school district?

Nicoloff Elementary looked exactly like Pence Elementary: semi-circle entry driveway, staff parking to the right, same office down to the furniture, identical outside halls, with columns on either side, classrooms set up the same, same yard with basketball courts out front.

It was always the same school.

I would teach one day at Nicoloff, then the next day at Pence, then the next at Nicoloff again, and I was like, "Where am I? I know this school and teachers, but who the hell am I?"

A Principal come into my classroom and I remembered that she had walked in on me the last time I was at this school, when my class had been in complete chaos.

15

This time there toys were strewn everywhere. Some students had a collection of bugs in a cup. The Principal said, "You better put that cup back and put those bugs outside."

"But the teacher said I could keep it," a little girl said.

"Sí, sí."

Usually, when a Principal came into my class, I got in trouble, not the kids. I was fired from an elementary school. At one school, another Substitute Teacher actually replaced me in the middle of my class.

It was hard for an individual student to get in trouble when streamers hung from the ceiling, dioramas kept spinning, and a paper wad fight would be going on. I had to stop blaming others for my shortcomings. I had wanted to be a Pied Piper, spouting wisdom and have all the students follow me. I knew I couldn't take it personally when they didn't.

I couldn't single out any student. When I said things that weren't guided by God, the kids would act as though I hadn't said anything at all. I began agreeing with them. Why should they pay attention to anyone but God?

I should have listened to other teachers who tried to give me advice on how to control a class. When I first started, a teacher told me, "You can't show fear. You have to believe in what you are telling them."

Fear was all over my face. I refused to bribe the kids with candy bars (one teacher's suggestion), and I couldn't keep threatening them with detention (another piece of advice). "I'm going to give them the choice to listen to me," I told myself, "or run rabid."

The kids chose the latter.

I kept chasing them in my classes, sometimes trying to get them to put down their chairs or dodging things thrown at me and others.

I remember substituting on a field trip. We took a bus to this historical site. Each teacher would get in front of the group to teach a small part of the lesson. The teacher who went before me had complete control of the class. When it was my turn, the children were fidgeting within seconds.

One little girl began to screech as if she couldn't stand to hear my voice. Seconds later, all the kids stood and would have run rampant if another teacher hadn't yelled, "Sit down and listen to him!"

This happened over and over to me. Every time it was my turn to teach, another teacher had to rescue me. Eventually, I stopped teaching the lessons and watched other teachers handle that for the rest of the day.

THE ASKER

Speculative Fiction

The best and worst six words in substituting are, "The children know what to do."

Sometimes you only have to say two initials, "A.R." and they work for an hour quietly without talking. But sometimes they say, "We're not supposed to do that today," and someone else will say, "Yes we are."

Then, during the course of the argument, a little girl might come up to you and say, "Teacher lets me write down the names of the people who are bad."

And then another child will say something like, "No, you ring the bell, like this."

And I might say, "Ok, we'll do this," but then the students will say, "No, we are not supposed to," and once this vortex has been opened, a group of students, about 10 at a time, will come up and ask questions at the same time:

"Can I go to the bathroom?"

"Can I get a drink?"

"Can I play on the computer?"

"Teacher said I had to go to the office for band money."

"Can I go with her to the bathroom?"

"Don't worry, Teacher, we're never this bad, Teacher."

"Consider the milk money collected, Teacher."

"Teacher, I wrote their names down, but my ears hurt!"

"Teacher, Tyrell hit me in the eye with a pencil."

"Teacher, well, is the answer yes or no?"

"I already did this work last time."

"Teacher lets me!"

And then I would find myself grabbing the bell and telling Stacy what names should go on the board.

This never worked. Kids would erase the chalkboard before the end of class.

The Principals and everyone in the disciplinary offices didn't want any part of me. I sent half of an entire middle school class to the office once, and they came back with a message from the Principal reminding me that I needed to control my class. Control, I was finding out, was something I didn't have.

A fellow teacher was thinking out loud in a teacher's lounge: "Teachers are playing with kids on the playground and losing their rapport with the students, and having a hard time controlling their classes."

I laughed because I never had any kind of rapport with my classes and not an ounce of control. So I had nothing to lose.

At recess with one class, the kids were gathered around me, and I was hitting the red rubber ball into the sky with my fist. I watched any semblance of control going high into the sky. There wasn't a cloud anywhere. That ball soared higher and higher. And when it would come down to the ground, the kids would yell, "Again! Again!" And I would punch the red ball again into the stratosphere.

I was the hero for a few minutes in my teaching career.

Teachers who were successful at keeping control of the class weren't necessarily angry at the kids. At the time, I thought I didn't yell at the kids enough. I thought, "I'm giving them the choice." If I yelled and forced them listen to me, wouldn't that be wrong?

Successful teachers got control by love.

I thought I was teaching with love, but had no idea what love was. Love wasn't something peachy keen where we would sings songs and the kids would follow me. Love wouldn't like to see others treating others badly. Love would stand firm on this. But I never wanted to cross that boundary. I was trying to make everyone like me at the same time I was trying to be an empathetic teacher.

The result was a quagmire – a quagmire of chaos.

WHAT? ONE OF THOSE SUBS

Walking back from lunch with fast food wrappers and a soda in my hands, I'd get that look from others teachers – *You're one of those Subs.* And it was true.

I rarely talked to anyone in the teacher's lounge. I ate out most of the time, and was usually shabbily dressed with messed up hair. I would occasionally sleep in my car in the parking lot during recess and before school started, and would play weird music as I drove by the students.

I remember asking one school secretary, "Doesn't this school look like another school? Or am I losing my mind?"

She looked through me over her glasses for a second, then resumed her posture of being frightened by the fact that I was a teacher.

A friend of mine echoed the same sentiment when he told my brother, "It's scary to think Andy is molding young minds."

That still scares me to this day.

I used to think dog ice cream and regular ice cream were the same thing.

In my parents' freezer, an ice cream treat with a dog on the front of the wrapper read, *Frosty Paws*. I tried it and thought, *This isn't the same thing*, while I was gagging. It said it was ice cream, but it tasted like dog food.

I thought of kids I've taught making this same mistake. I was training them to eat dog food.

I didn't even know the nursery rhymes the way I should. I would teach the wrong verses to songs and the kids would get them all mixed up. Worse, they would miss the lessons the songs were supposed to teach.

Sometimes I woke up ready to scream: "The Itsy Bitsy Spider! I'm a little teapot short and stout, not *spout*. Now the Itsy Bitsy Spider will never find its way out. You might as well tip me over and pour me out!"

My mom was a nursery school teacher. She packed the trunk of her car with musical toys that played songs and nursery rhymes. Once my brother was driving her car and got pulled over by a cop. And the trunk was playing all these songs. My brother looked at the cop and shrugged his shoulders.

We were raised with those songs. But I sometimes felt like the Mad Hatter when I would leave after teaching a class. I remember one teacher's aide looking at me and laughing as I walked along singing one of those songs.

THE
POLVERING

I woke up feeling sick, not having slept the night before due to a cough and fever. I decided right away that there was no way I was capable of working. When I called the Sub Desk, of course it was too late to cancel through the computer.

That day, the first-grade class pulverized me. It ranked up there with some of the worst experiences of my life. I left a note – *A living nightmare* – and left. Later, in a bookstore with two second-grade workbooks in my hand, I felt my stare pierce the bookcases, and knew that if someone had said something to me, I could not have answered them. I don't know what kept those workbooks in my hand: *"Put the weapon down, Susie. Put the weapon down."*

So many times, other teachers would come into my class to say, "Listen to Andy . He's an adult." The kids wouldn't buy it. The minute that other teacher would leave, a wrestling bell might as well have sounded: pandemonium.

I didn't see it as humiliating that other teachers had to convince the kids that I was an adult. I explained this to a friend who expected me to feel embarrassed. "I would be embarrassed," I told him, "but my nerves are shot."

Embarrassing moments don't define us. Humiliating ones do.

21

In one P.E. class I taught — achieving a new level of chaos, even for me — there were no walls holding the children in. They could scamper around and tackle each other on the pavement and basically run riot. The minute I began to speak, bedlam exploded.

Called to the Principal's office, I was told I would never teach at that school again. I went straight to a thrift store and bought a used P.E. shirt from a middle school. On the back in block letters: *Always dress in your P.E. uniform. Obey all safety rules. Run in an orderly fashion. Attitude is everything.*

Even if that P.E. class and that school had rejected me, I could still be part of the team.

A t Disneyland with my cousin and her two children, a boy and a girl both under 11 years old, we went inside the Princess Castle. The character Belle came over to our table and my cousin's daughter posed with her for a photo, but her brother darted in to spoil picture on purpose. Belle told him "OK, now I will take a picture with you."

The boy yelled, "No!" But Belle drew him close. He raised his arms to hide his face in shame. It was a great photograph, one I still own. The feeling that 10-yearold had summed up my feelings as a Substitute Teacher.

B eing a Substitute Teacher always made me feel the same way I did when I shopped at a craft store over Christmas: demoralized. The whole time, I could see the front of the line. It just wasn't moving.

Four-foot poles stuck out of the shopping carts. People inched forward like drones, shuffling, heads down. When customers finished paying, they moved toward the exit door, their heads still down. Suddenly, they would be shocked awake by a *Slam!* Looking up from their daze, they would see that metal pole preventing them from leaving the store with their carts. In that moment, the cashier loved to shout, "Merry Christmas!"

Sometimes I wondered how I ever got out of that store. Or those classrooms.

4

"I'M LINE LEADER"

"TEACHER, HE CUTTED"

"TEACHER SAYS I'M LINE LEADER
I'M STUDENT OF THE WEEK

"THAT WAS LAST WEEK"

"TEACHER, HE CUTTED, I ALWAYS

LEAD THE LINE"

"HE'S GOT TO GO TO THE BACK
OF THE LINE, TEACHER SAYS"

"I'M TELLING THE TEACHER"

"YOU ALWAYS CUT"

"TEACHER, YOU HAVE TO PUT HIS
NAME ON THE BOARD.
TEACHER SAYS."

My lines through the hallway baffled my colleagues. Kids in front would take off running around the corner. I'd be stuck standing in the middle of the line, looking back at the end of it, which always moved slowly. Inevitably I would have to return to the classroom to find one child still putting stuff away.

"Hurry up," I'd tell her or him, knowing that most of my class was running like terror through the school.

"Just a second, I just have to put his away," the student would tell me. "And this."

Pacing back and forth, I had to laugh at myself. Most schools have a strict policy of straight, silent lines — and then my class comes around the corner and almost takes out Mrs. Johnson and her orderly crew. My class would never listen when I called out to the front of the line. Since I don't believe in threats and bribes, I got my butt kicked even harder.

I was also supposed to follow the posted rules and say, "Ut-oh, stay off the grass." On duty as the grass protector after school, I was supposed to stand with a bullhorn and yell at students 10 feet in front of me if they walked on a 20 square-foot patch of grass. I never said anything – even when I was being paid to. Besides, I would have been laughing too hard to manage it.

N ow that I look back on it, I wonder, "Why didn't I just get in front of the line?"
Even if I had, the kids would probably have scattered in another direction.

There can be nothing more revered in Elementary School than the coveted position of line leader. A line leader got chosen by the Permanent Teacher. It might take weeks, even months for kids paying their dues in the hard knocks middle-of-the-line to be deemed worthy of being called line leader. They would never have honored me as their line leader. They would have rebelled. In their eyes, I wasn't qualified to be a hall monitor.

Driving back to college, my friend and I had gone to another town, about two hours away. Later that night, we drove on to our college town, pulled over to the side of the road and slept. A police flashlight hitting our window woke us up. The policeman asked where we were heading. I told him "We're on our way back to Sacramento."

The officer was a jolly guy: "Sacramento is four hours in the other direction."

No wonder the kids didn't want to follow me. Even I didn't want to follow me.

It all came down to the question of qualifications:

- I told a class in Imperial Beach that the Coronado Bridge was a suspension bridge. (It's not.) I got corrected five times by the same fifth-grader who had been acing subtraction on the board.
- Teaching a packet of kindergarten Spanish, one little girl smoked me. She actually knew Spanish.
- I lost at Tic-Tac-Toe. A lot.
- One kid got five in a row on me one time in a game of Connect Four.

- Another kid with the goosiest moves I had ever seen took me down in Duck-Duck-Goose, and made me sit in the middle of the class, where kids called others names and made fun of them. In Spanish.

SAVE THE KIDDIES

As a kid, I had a cousin who was a sleepwalker. One time she woke up in a neighbor's yard more than an acre away. That's how I felt as a Substitute Teacher — someone would wake me up one in the middle of my class and say, "You were sleepwalking into this chemistry class, claiming you could teach chemistry. Hilarious!"

I realized that it took more energy to conserve energy than to expend it. Adults might have similar amounts of energy as children if they did everything with all of their hearts, the way children do. The problem for me was that I had nowhere near that level of heart back then, so students would run circles around me.

I tried to control them. I stopped kids from leaving the class, but they would just slip out a different door. I'd send students to the office, but they would run wild in the halls instead. I would write a note to the permanent teacher, and the kids would steal it. I'd write their names on the board. They'd erase it.

So used to having no control over my classes, I was shocked whenever it seemed that students were actually listening to me.

One girl in the front row once got control of the class for me in less than five seconds. Then she looked at me and said, "OK. Now teach."

I stood there thinking, *Teach what?"*

My one shot at control had evaporated as quickly as it had appeared. Pandemonium erupted again.

I n a Special Ed class, I had to shadow one student around. He kept repeating my name — "AAAndeeee" — like the star of *Pee Wee's Big Adventure*. The whole time, he ran around the campus, jumping off trash cans, knocking things over.

In another Special Ed class, the kids responded well to me. For the first time I thought, *Maybe this is the direction I should go.* A Teacher's Aide saw the same thing: "You work well with them. Most other teachers come in with an agenda and something to say, but you don't."

And I thought, *Yeah, I'm good at that no-agenda, nothing-to-say stuff.*

Toward the end of my career as a Substitute Teacher, I established a curriculum of my own design. I had become so used to students not listening to me for more than a few seconds, I had stopped trying. Then I decided, "I will get learning packets."

At KMART, in the teaching section, I bought packets for children to fill out. One of the packets had a picture of a desk with a chair on top of it. Students had to write what was wrong with each picture. I showed that packet to a friend and she said, "Why can't there be a chair on top of a desk? It's crazy what we are teaching our kids."

She's right, I thought — our KMART packet-based curriculum contained no mystery. We were teaching kids about certainty, but we weren't certain about the things we were teaching.

I wrote a prose poem about this outrage:

65 Million Year Old Crime Solved

A mother Hadrasaur was found slain on Monday. Forensic Scientists say the victim's fossil was found near Lake Michigan. Forensic Scientists say what is most vile about the crime is that the corpse was buried in the pre-cretaceous level of the Earth's crust, millions of years before the Hadrasaur's period.

There are many suspects: Laelaps, Brachiasaurus, Velociraptor among them. Who had the motive? Scientists   wondered. But Forensic Scientists have conclusive evidence that it was Archeopteryx who committed the crime. It was Archeopteryx who slashed the Hadrasaur's throat with its talons.

And the Hadrasaur struck back with a bite to the wing. This was considered self-defense, since Archeopteryx had just stolen the Hadrasaur's egg and Archeopteryx did in fact kill her.

The descendents of the Hadrasaur, which include the flamingo and the platypus, can finally rest knowing justice has been served.

Descendents of Archeopteryx were taken into custody Monday. "I never trusted Archeopteryx", one policeman said. Scientists were able to reenact the entire scene thanks to the shape of Archeopteryx's head, which proved it did this sort of thing and hibernated in trees in winter.

Scientists were also able to conclude from its head that Archeopteryx lived like a flying squirrel, jumping from tree to tree.

There is said to be a mini-series coming out on TNT, titled, *An Archeopteryx Stole My Baby*.

I t felt as if I was trying to explain time zones to a really stupid child. In my mind, there are no stupid children, only those smart and willing to fight the ridiculous things they're being taught. I read that politicians might pass a law to end Daylight Savings Time. The *Maximum Weather Leadership* my local news station could offer might make it seem as though the sun was obeying that law. *And today would be a good day to try Lipitor—now with Lutein.*

It wasn't as though I didn't try my best to keep control of my classes. I starting to speak to one class, and a kid ran up to me wide-eyed and said, "Yeah! We've got this guy!" He started throwing things. The rest of the class joined him.

I had three different classes in different school districts that all said the minute I started speaking, "You're the teenager on *Family Guy!*" Chaos followed each time.

I was beginning to find out that my best wasn't good enough.

When I first moved to the West Coast as a Junior High student, I didn't know anyone. I ate lunch by myself, sitting in the grass while everyone else gathered in groups. That was the worst sunlight I ever experienced.

It felt as if everyone was watching me. Not long after that, I found a group – not to join, but to follow. At lunch, this group would walk around campus. I'd hang in the back, shuffling my feet. When someone would say something to me, I would mumble words that couldn't be understood. I sought fellowship in order to hide. I was a follower in the worst sense of the word.

As a Substitute Teacher, I was still a follower. I followed to hide, but found no place to hide in. I stood alone in the brutal sunlight again, and I wanted cover so badly.

Being exposed to that harsh light helped me to stop hiding. At first, I had the *If you can't beat them – join them* mentality. But I couldn't really join them. I wasn't accepted. That was painful. Then I decided to stop following, to stop hiding, and to start writing down my experiences. And to start loving the kids I was there to teach.

I wasn't ready to be a leader, but I refused to follow. And I still couldn't get out of the way of the paper wads. It was time to make a Substitute's Last Stand: *This paper wad is for the children!*

At a High School called Gompers, I thought about leaving the Substitute life: a single paper wad thrown and Gompers would be gone. *Go, Go, Gompers! Go, Go, Gompers!* Changed by the unforgiving light, I felt less afraid than ever. It was time to move on.

I didn't sign off dramatically, like our Founding Fathers, with a pen name like Publius. No one really knew who I was. I just stopped showing up. I officially cancelled my Substitute Teacher license with the districts. Subfinder could no longer find me.

I was no longer Mr. P.

I had tried my best to control the classes I taught. Out of that failed attempt came a teaching style that could still be taught to teachers everywhere to this day. My inspiration came from Otto, the bus driver on *The Simpsons*: "Put on your seat belts."

"We don't have seat belts."

"Well just try to go limp."

I explained my philosophy to a friend: "I've been teaching for over a year now – and not a single proven fatality."

THE TIME BETWEEN

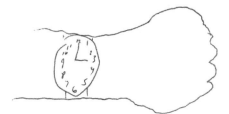

subbed for about a year. Not allowed in many schools anymore, I could have kept going, but I was battered and beaten. This warrior longed for home.

I moved in with my parents, out of the area. I held some odd jobs (I didn't really hold them — got fired from most of them). I started drinking heavily on the weekends.

On those nights, I would go to an Irish bar down the street and spend the evening senselessly rambling on about anything and everything. One night *Snow Dogs: the Movie* was on TV at the bar. It starred Cuba Gooding, Jr. whose arctic sled dogs talk. It wasn't a cartoon. It was a live-action movie, with poor special effects. I began telling everyone in the bar, "Snow Dogs is a true story. Those dogs can really talk."

I went on and on in a senseless diatribe, the kind in the *Saturday Night Live* skit *Superstar*, with Molly Shannon, playing a young girl at a talent show, rambling on, then throwing her hands in the air and yelling, "Monologue!"

I didn't get a single date with a woman that whole time. I didn't make a single friend. I did heavily abuse alcohol.

I threw up once with such force that capillaries in my face burst. My face turned black. I wrote a poem about it, titled, *My Face Died So I Bought a Giant Tennis Ball.*

At the time, I was thinking about going the Special Ed teacher route. A woman I met at that bar told me she was studying sign language. I said, "Really! I am interested in the field!"

She kept talking and signing as she spoke. We talked for a bit and I finally confessed that I didn't speak sign language. She kept signing as we talked for the next 10 minutes. I convinced myself I was drunk enough to understand it.

Talk about being lost. At this stage in my life, I felt less a person, more a performance artist. I was a mime who could talk – actually, a mime who wouldn't shut up.

I joked about my problem with alcohol. A trainer at a gym had me write what I ate each day on the strict diet he had me on. I wrote: *10 Guinness, two sausage pancakes on a stick.*

With that diet, I finally got arrested for driving under the influence. It was the best thing that ever happened to me.

I had been trying to be extra careful, driving two miles an hour when I was pulled over. It was the grace of God.

At trial, the Prosecutor asked, "So let me get this straight, you had seven beers?"

"Seven pints," I corrected.

Her eyes widened. "OK! Seven *pints*!"

Even after that exchange, God kept protecting me. The hung jury (six voting Guilty, six Not Guilty) produced a conviction on a lesser charge. I still remember my lawyer saying, "Seven *pints* and you still hung the jury. You should go in the *Guinness Book of Records.*"

God was moving in my life. That forced me to reevaluate things.

There is nothing funny about drunk driving. I would be telling a much different story if I had hurt someone. I can only attest to the mercy of God.

Once again, God did not give me what I deserved. I got the penalty of a DUI, but without the charge. It ended up costing me about $10,000, and I had to go to classes three times a week. I lost my driver's license for a year. It could have been a lot worse.

Arrested, I spent 14 hours in the drunk tank. Those were hard hours. A friend later mocked me about it: "Try doing two years!"

For over a year, I remained essentially under house arrest, without a driver's license. I became productive in writing. I wrote a story that I felt God gave me. It was a comedy.

But comedy, as it pertained to Godliness, was (and is) something rare. Most comic movies have some dark agenda. They make it seem as if comedy comes from doing drugs and living a life with no morals. But I believed—and believe now—comedy comes from God.

There seem to be two kinds of comedy movies: the Goody-Two-Shoes type, where everyone has been inhaling from a canister of fake love, and the Dark Agenda style, where humor comes from breaking down barriers or morals, with shocking dialog. Only rarely were there *clean* comedies that weren't fake and didn't have a dark agenda.

When I worked at a movie theater, I caught two minutes of one movie. In that brief time, the movie had reinforced a variety of stereotypes, presented a brutal agenda and hit me as deeply dishonest. Yet people left the theater saying, "That was cute."

Since I felt that God gave me my comedy story, I was keen on giving God the glory for it. I wanted to publish it anonymously. On the back cover, in place of a picture of the author, I wanted a picture of a pencil.

At this period of my life, I was interested in opening an art gallery called *God*. No artist would get credit for the art. God would get all of it. After all, God was responsible for the good in this world, but got none of the credit. This was so noble and true of me, it made me feel like a prophet.

I confused identities with God. So many of my realizations and theories made people shake their heads and say, "Of course not." I missed the obvious. Pride is a funny thing. It gets stronger the more you fight it. Letting go of pride, not fighting it, was the answer.

That's why I had been led to becoming a Substitute Teacher and to be humiliated.

31

With this insight, I wrote cover letters for my stories, submitted them to hundreds of publishers, all of whom rejected me. I created an advertisement for one story, feeling certain that it should be published unedited.

Pumpkin and Fluffernutter
by Andrew Palasciano

Scandalous!
  Completely Unedited!
    With Misspelled Words!

My name is Andrew Palasciano and I tried real hard at writing this story but then I remembered you can't tie someone to a chair, beat the crap out of them 'til they tell you what you want to know, then call yourself Wonder Woman.

My career in advertising didn't work out.

A good life, like good art, is a clean glass that God can pour His Spirit into.
A clean vessel is a humble vessel. God humbles us through humiliation and shame.

When I was a kid, we had a beach house with a lake next to some dunes. It had a dock in the back yard, on the lake. I would fall off that dock into the lake so often that my mom laid out two sets of clothes for me each day.

Once, a little girl threw a crab trap into the water and knocked me limp and into the lake.

Even now, I don't know how I survived that body of water.

Collage makers sometimes find a *live* page. It may be in a newspaper or a book, an art book – anything. This page seems to crackle with electricity, like being a kid with a jar of fireflies in a lightning storm.

God sends a charge through a clean vessel that He has created and that charge runs down your leg, just like when I was such a chronic bed wetter so badly that my mom bought a shock blanket that would wake me up.

Another wake-up call came while riding in the backseat of a station wagon. I was eight years old, with my friend — a girl from down the block — sitting next to me. The car made a sharp turn and my door swung open. I watched the road going by underneath us. Feeling a charge go through me, I leaned out of the car, my hair blowing in the breeze. I felt like a hero: *I'm going to close this door and save everyone here.*

I grabbed the handle, my head and torso hovering above the moving road. Then I lost my grip and tumbled out.

After I stopped rolling, I saw the station wagon still driving away. Finally, it stopped and came back to get me. I still remember my mom holding fingers in front of my face: "How many fingers am I holding up?"

Loopy, and still holding onto my dreams of being a hero, I answered, "Yes."

Then I got carried home.

A lot of us think that if God could actually guide us, we should hit a home run every time. But God can guide us to strike out, too.

And to fall out of moving cars.

P laying kickball at recess on gravelly concrete, I got a turn to kick. I had stars in my eyes, wanting to kick that ball over the school and into the street. The pitcher rolled the ball, I looked up to the spot I wanted to kick it to – out in the netherworld. I completely missed the ball.

Worse, my kicking motion sent me the ground and dragged my kicking leg along the rugged cement, giving me a bloody raspberry that covered my entire thigh.

A few days later, a friend joked, "I'm going to stab your leg there with a knife."

I cringed. That would not only have been unspeakably painful, it would have been a dagger in my already wounded pride.

Most people think they can do things without God. They hear how talented they are. Talents vary, but only God can determine the extent of anyone's abilities.

Art provided a good example for me. In a painting contest between someone with $50-million talent who was not guided by God, and another person with less talent, but guided by God, the high-priced talent would lose. It wouldn't even be close.

Being *creative* is a misnomer. I didn't *create* anything. There is only one Creator, and we did not create Him or anything He has made. God gives us clean vessels that He can use, but by ourselves, we are not *creative*.

If being a Substitute Teacher taught me anything, it's that there is only one genius in this universe. (Hint: it's not me.)

I thought I was a chef, but I was just the dinner plate. These days, I can be a clean plate that God can use to serve a great meal on. But I didn't make the meal.

I got so sure of vessels, I would tell someone, "This is a great album. It's so powerful!" Listening to it the next day, that album might do nothing for me. God can use the album, but the album itself has no power.

I'd feel embarrassed after telling everyone the album was so great. Then I would realize it wasn't the music that had moved me. It was God. My life was like that: I'd get so sure of myself, then see that I have never been sure of anything.

My mom made me a Halloween costume to wear to nursery school: a full body black leotard and a backpack made to look like the giant shell of a lady bug. At school, someone called me a lady bug. I threw off the backpack and yelled, "I'm not a lady!"

I ran around all day with nothing on but a black leotard.

As a kid, I thought I was stronger than any girl. Then I got shown in a hurry that I wasn't strong. But I fought against the obvious and tried to talk my way out of a proverbial paper bag. I wrote a poem about this: *The Armless Boxer Who Fought with His Tongue.*

As a young man, I had my foot in my mouth all the time, sometimes my whole leg. Then God began to show me that winning in life depends not only on what we say, but what we don't say.

I was proud of my strength and I talked proudly. In elementary school, the teacher set up a camera, aimed at a desk. Students had to look into the camera and report a news story, like a TV news anchor. When my turn came around, I glared into the lights and froze, unable to think of a word to say. I squirmed, absolutely terrified. After 10 seconds, the female student next to me at the desk read my lines. I hid.

I remember the class laughing when we watched the video of our news show. I couldn't fight my way out of a corner with my tongue. I now knew better, but it didn't stop me from getting slapped down again and again as I kept fighting against myself. I wrote a poem about this, too: *Trench Foot of the Tongue.*

This condition lasted into my working career. We work to get what we need to live and love. I worked to make my interactions after work risk free. I was still hiding.

I used to try to improve my looks with exercise and conformity clothing. I got treated like everyone else. But I knew I was different. I still had my membership card to a video store from when I was a kid, didn't I?

I remember renting James Bond movies with my brother, proving the store slogan: *Membership has its privileges.* When that video store was up for sale, my brother's co-worker, a woman in her early 20's, reacted with surprise: "They still have those?"

Most people her age had never been inside a video store, the same way many people my age and older don't understand texting. I took a class on texting. On a list of 100 texting abbreviations, I knew nine. One texting phrase I learned that first day made me feel out of place, alone: *yoyo* – you're on your own. But God never left me alone. He has always been there, even in my most dramatic failures – especially the comical ones

On a high school ski trip, the leader was a much better skier than the rest of us. He took us to a massive jump from a 20-foot boulder, with a flat landing zone. Several guys went before me. A few crashed, some made it. Showing off, the leader did a mid-air body-twisting trick, landing it perfectly. Then my turn.

Nervous, I hurried my start. Pushing off the jump, sailing through the sky, I spotted a skier before me whose crash had stuck him in the landing spot. My landing spot.

I tried grabbing the back of my skis to pull a fakey (I'm not sure that's what it's called). I came down on my face, just missing my friend who had crashed. The guys who had already landed all started laughing. The leader came over to make sure I was OK. Once again, it was mostly my pride that hurt.

A fter I'd wet my own bed, I would crawl into my sister's bed. She was always there for me. Her room stood above a roof. A wind would blow in the trees. Those nights felt timeless.

We would dress up like *Raggedy Ann* and *Andy* (her name is Anne). She had those dolls in our play room. That room had a red rug. I was more dreamer than boy back then, so much into my own world that I wasn't in the real one.

At the Boys Club, my brother Ed and I would play Wiffle Ball on a field with a wall, just like a regular baseball park. Home runs would land on a hill over that wall. It was a special place, the perfect size for kids like us.

Our version of Wiffle Ball allowed us throw the ball at base runners: hit them with the ball when they weren't on the base and they were out. Once, when Ed and I played softball on another field – I remember it being a bright day, and I remember dreaming with the trees – I caught a grounder at shortstop. A base runner ran by me on his way to third. I threw that heavy ball, hitting him square in the back. He came at me, yelling. My brother stepped in: "He's used to Wiffle Ball. He doesn't know any better."

And I didn't. All I knew was the trees were swaying in bright sunlight and I had caught a ground ball. The real world had collided with mine.

lived from the inside out too much as a child. Around age 14, I started to be concerned with how I looked. I became obsessive. Seeing others interact, I'd think, *I would have said it this way, not that way.*

I would also imagine unreal social scenarios, practicing vain and phony facial expressions. I grew more and more fake, becoming arrested in adolescence. I grew in reverse direction for years. It has taken me 20 years to get close to the person I've always been – 20 years to start living from the inside-out again.

Living from the outside-in frustrated me. I actually became more introverted because I was planning what to say and trying to control how everyone would react. When I was fake, defense was offense, offense was defense. This left me alone, swimming in the deep end.

I would find out that I was not alone.

Visiting my brother at his condo, someone in the unit above him made a lot of noise with his footsteps. I imagined going up there one day, knocking on the door, and confronting an old man who wore the same shoes as the band Kiss did on stage – two-foot long spikes on the soles – making the guy seven feet tall.

That image reminded me of a day when a friend took us to the house of someone he claimed he knew. There was no one home. We played pool and wore these Viking helmets that we found lying around. When the owner came home, our friend tried to hide. He had no idea who this man was. My brother tried to save the day: "It's OK, we're Vikings."

For a second, I believed him. That was how fake I was back then.

I seemed to be true, even to myself, but it was an illusion. When my friend's new printer stopped working, he and his girlfriend called the printer company. They argued for an hour about how they had been sold a printer that didn't work.

Finally, a manager got on the phone and said, "We have what's called the Best Effort Policy." This basically meant that the company tried to make a reliable printer, but because it didn't work, my friend couldn't get his money back. The company had tried its best.

That summed up the effectiveness of my fake behavior. No matter how hard I tried, My Best Effort Policy didn't cut it.

My brother Dan had a job once that even I couldn't get fired from. He was a car counter. He stood on a street corner and counted how many cars drove by. "But how would your boss know how many cars drove by?" I asked. That instantly sounded like a challenge – and I love a challenge. I've been fired from jobs that gave me much less to work with.

In my poem, *Lanyard* (a strap that goes around the neck to hold a badge, a key – anything too valuable to lose), I described my whole career. I had a light strap around my neck, so light that it was like wearing a watch. After a while I didn't notice I was wearing it.

That was the opposite of having an albatross around my neck. One of my favorite parts of a *Monty Python* episode showed a vendor at a stadium, walking up the aisle with a giant white bird in the merchandise box hanging from his shoulders. The bird's wings spread five feet on either side of him. He's hawking, "Albatross!"

I had something hanging from my shoulders. I just couldn't feel what it was.

My old voice mail message: "This is Andy. I'm not here. Leave a message after the tone."

A friend left this message: "You're not where?"

I hadn't thought about it, not really. It reminded me of one message I got from a someone in an office in Minnesota:

"Hi Grant. Just getting some coffee and I will be back at my desk in two minutes."

I saved that message. I felt I had to.

Years later, a friend dressed up for Halloween as a Smart and Final employee named Grant. All night he kept introducing himself: "Hi, Welcome to Smart and Final. I'm Grant, can I help you?"

I still have that message in my voice mail.

wanted to be a righteous man. The only problem: I've never been right and God has never been wrong.

The only times I've been "right" is when God guides me to the truth. I have never had an idea that didn't come from God. But I wanted a silhouette painted of me – a picture with head turned sideways, as if everything was my idea, not God's. My silhouette was more like the chalk lines around a dead body on the pavement. My ideas never got me anywhere but lost.

I remember going on a fishing trip with a lunchbox my parents packed for me. It was silver and shiny. I held it up and told everyone on the boat, "I'm going to space camp!"

And while we were fishing, someone next to me hooked a yellowtail. He reeled in what looked like a dinosaur coming up out of the sea. Turns out, it was a 600-pound sunfish that had just eaten the yellowtail on that line. Thirty seconds later, a deck hand came over and cut the line, saving the rod and reel.

Years later, I listened to a live radio show on fishing when a fisherman hooked a sunfish and saw it come out of the water. He started crying: "It's a baby wheel!" ("whale" in an New England accent).

I totally related to this reaction. That fish did look prehistoric.

And by this time, I finally knew that sometimes we catch what we never expected.

6

I DID MY BANKING AT 7-11

The first time I ever heard the word *convenience*, I was just a kid. A nearby storefront, similar to a liquor store, stood dark. But neon lights filled the window: *Convenience Store*. It had a video game, *Millipede*, and my cousins and I played it a few times.

When I first saw a microwave, I said, "You can choose how long it will take to heat up something?" And I reasoned, *If it's up to me, why not choose for it to take one second to heat up what you put in it?* Why would anyone choose to wait a minute when the food could be ready in a second?

This level of convenience should be the norm, I thought. And I thought it was already possible. I was about to discover, the space age couldn't live for me.

There was also a Flea Market by our house in Rhode Island. On bright sunny Sundays, people would come from all over the country to sell their Motley Crue shirts and patches, as well as old paintings, antiques and all sorts of knick knacks. God let me enjoy wandering through these things. I even bought patches for my Little League jacket. But just as a husband doesn't buy his wife candy so she'll fall in love with candy, but with him, God didn't want me to fall in love with these flea market items, but with Him.

A lake in Connecticut we used to visit had floating docks that we could swim out to. There were crayfish for catching and bugs in the light at night. The ice cream man would drive to that lake in the evening and kids would mob his truck. I always bought a Patriot Pop, with red, white and blue stripes. (This was the original, long before Freedom Fries.)

By a beach in Rhode Island, we used to eat clam cakes at the Little Red Store. Sometimes they were sandy clam cakes, but they were good. It was here that, for the first time, I saw someone steal.

My childhood friend stole a candy bar. On the long walk back to our house, I got over my shock.

We'd go crabbing and clamming. Once, a huge jellyfish floated in from the ocean. Our friend cut it to pieces with his clam rake. He and my brother got stung all over their legs.

Another time, my brother was water skiing. Showing off, he put the handle of the tow rope in his teeth. There was a jelly fish on that handle. His whole mouth got stung.

So, I had an enchanted childhood. I walked with God and loved God. It felt like a dream, one I was pulled out of. Actually, I pulled myself out of that dream. I fell in love with things (the candy) instead of with God.

Around adolescence, the stage of life that one writer called *the time between*, I lost my way. This writer noted that the imagination of both a child and a man are healthy, it's that time between those stages that was troublesome. I've been between those two stages for longer than I spent in my childhood. If I infect others with trouble, it's only because I need to express where I'm at.

So – sorry about that.

I was working against becoming a man. To me, being a man meant hurting people and taking pleasure in it. Violence (I was jumped once in college – that was once too many), joking, humiliating others, then laughing about it. I hated *guy talk* and didn't want to become *a man*. So, I went my own way.

This path led to uncharted territory. Unable to follow my heart, I believed the heart was a deceiver. I could almost see the Scarecrow from *The Wizard of Oz* with his arms pointing in both directions.

When someone is pure, he thinks he'll never become corrupt. When he's corrupt, he thinks he'll never become pure. It was that way with me for a long time. I felt defiled by so many things, and that robbed all of the true joy from my life. Whenever I momentarily escaped that state, I started to believe that the source of my defilement was also the source of my joy. It felt like drowning, then coming up for air—the air tastes great. I learned that the drowning wasn't the source of joy. The air was. God was my air, and I felt compelled to drown.

> Drowning doesn't make a man a hero,
> and God cracked the bowl and left me
> swimming for The Kingdom of Zero.

I had to reach the bottom to look up and realize that God had been my air the whole time. He has been my joy. I could live in that joy all the time. I didn't need to needlessly drown.

What I learned: don't make a gift a chore.

I used to view busy work as a bad thing. Shopping for groceries and going to the bank were annoyances. This was why I did my banking at 7-11. The problem wasn't the busy work. The problem was that I was corrupt. Things that are gifts when you are pure are not gifts when you are corrupt.

Some of my most joyous moments now happen when I'm doing busy work. Before that, I tried to free myself from busy work so I'd be free to party. I now know from Job Coaching that having your hands busy with the wrong things, like eating and drinking to excess, can breed a type of insanity that turns a gift into a chore. Then you're only really free to hurt someone.

I'm a low-key guy and I don't do well in most social settings. But going out to events where there is nothing to do drove me insane. That's why I liked my brother and his friends, who would play Wiffle Ball and basketball. Being with them was a gift, not a chore. Life wasn't something that you had to do, but something you got to do.

Seems simple but, at the time, I thought I was so righteous that I didn't need to keep my hands busy with good things. I could do good things without God, and labeled myself as the secretary in *Ferris Bueller's Day Off* described the hero: "He's a righteous dude."

Of course, I was no collection of righteous acts. I was a person — something I tried to avoid being by hiding. I hid by trying to become everything, even God. I did everything in my power to be everything but who I was.

So I kept running, thinking I was in the lead and going to win this race, and it would be "Michelob Light for the Winner." But I wasn't racing against anyone but myself, and running away from everyone else.

Trouble found me every day. It was torment. Trouble and corruption go hand-in-hand. I had to learn to come to God when I was corrupt and in trouble. This proved hard for me. I was *a righteous dude.*

Pride was the root of my trouble, but fear came along with it, making it a game. There is even a board game called *Trouble*. It has dice in a little plastic glass dome that you click and the dice spin. It's exciting, like *Jenga!* (except you say "Trouble!"). In my adventure, piloting my space ship named *Trouble*, I headed into uncharted territories. Instead, I flew back to my heart, where I was sick and going nowhere.

I went lower, got sicker, and more quicksand waited for me. I was under the delusion that I was swimming and carrying the whole world to dry land. I suffered the cold ocean for the children, so I could bring them to Paradise. I really felt that people should buy my video tape on how I led them home, so future generations would know exactly how I did it.

In this future, everyone would be safe. I would be this great hero, immortalized in poetry and song. My phony humility saw this as an unfortunate side effect for a greater purpose: saving mankind. But I was the one who needed saving.

Swimming in quicksand, I had no branch to hold on to, but I was deluded enough to think I could jump into quicksand, save everyone, and survive.

43

No hero, I wasn't even an anti-hero. I was a young man drowning in his own delusions. It never occurred to me that I could love and be loved. Life was more complicated than that, I thought, and I would figure it out so everyone could be happy. I didn't realize I was playing a *Monty Python* character who says to King Arthur, "What should we do now – run away farther?"

When someone would call me a good guy, I wanted to say, "Don't judge me!" Calling me a good guy did more harm than good because some part of me truly believed that.

And I would bring all my friends down with me. I'd have these deep conversations that troubled everyone but me. I thought I was so wise. In a poem, I described how I was drowning, with my friends paddling out in a life raft to save me:

> I pull them in the water, step on their heads,
> then climb into the raft and pull them up again,
> laughing and calling myself Fisher of Men.

I had been cowering since childhood – cowering with kindness, handing out honors so I could receive honor in return. I was fishing for compliments, not a Fisher of Men. But God mercifully let me make CDs, including one called *War of the Tuna Fish*, and let me think I would catch compliments and honors with my fishing pole, things that never came and, thankfully, never will.

I gave up fishing and started farming. Farmers know the sun and rain make fruit. Anything a farmer might make himself would be inedible. Friends might demand fruit, eat the fake fruit and say, "It's not his best fruit, but at least he made fruit." And the farmer could only throw the rest of his fake fruit in the fire and wait for the real harvest.

I like fruit, by the way. Real fruit. Peaches are my favorite.

A client/friend I go with to the movies and to dinner likes to walk around and talk to people. Sometimes he'll say hello as if he knew the person. "You know her? I'd ask.

"She was my Job Coach," he told me. "Almost."

Art isn't like that. In art, there is no *almost*. It's true or it isn't. It was made by God or it wasn't.

Late in life, facing declining royalties from his *Wizard Of Oz* books, Frank Baum, wrote the seventh in the series, *The Patchwork Girl of Oz*. I don't know if it's good or not – Baum thought it was one of the best two books he had ever written – but it didn't reverse the decline in sales of the series. That made me think: how much art have I tried to do out of convenience or need or just to make a point, instead of waiting for God?

When I learned to depend on God, I stopped drowning. *You the bobber, I the robber*, was how I described it. God was my buoy, leading me to write, *The stars were held up with sticks like chop suey, then the sun came out buoy.*

When you float, the ocean doesn't seem so intimidating. And at night, this buoy might fill with helium and soar into the night sky.

A friend who grew up on a farm described what happened with his mules: "They got in the meadow and got unbroke." This was how I felt with God carrying me. At the time, I wrote: *The broken horse is wild.* With God's wind in the sails of my ship, I could go anywhere. I went on to write: *I picked up a fish and it smiled.* I was happy to be floating and flying.

I wrote a poem back then, describing a ceremony of my succeeding in becoming a man. Soldiers shot into the sky as Maniac Crow Man (me) bowed. The soldiers said, "You have been humbled." I believed that becoming a man would happen all at once in some ceremony. (I was right about one thing: I was a maniac.)

I owned a picture of birds, with one bird entering a flock of thousands. That's how I thought it would be when I became a man: I'd enter the whole group and there would be a checkered flag. In my story *Tablecloth*, an endless table sat in the sun with red and yellow checkered tablecloths and napkins. But everything is backwards inside a cyclone. A kettle of hawks (really, that's what it's called) circles in the distance. I enter as one of thousands.

Maniac Crow Man had a lot to learn.

I often wondered, "What is Jabberwocky?" I thought of Iceland, where horses lived in snow. I loved to listen to Icelandic singers. Did I understand it? It was like a baby talking its own language. They gave speeches: "Fix the broken shudder."

45

At a table set with salad forks, Alice is having tea. She can't control growing bigger or smaller. They sing a song backwards. Flowers seem to be speaking back to them.

In a picture I drew, titled *Dimestore Philosophy*, a wheel got pounded by a storm: lightning over the ocean, rain leaking into a cottage by the beach. Inside, two men played gin rummy at a table sitting on pillars. The Cheshire Cat's face was twirling outside, bouncing from window to window like a pogo stick. The card players did not look up. Their gaze was focused on something beyond.

My drawing skill is still about fifth grade level, so not everything made it into the picture. But my skill level fit this picture because it was about that time in my life: when I was in 5th grade we moved across the country. I remember driving past the Woolworth's as we left our home town. And I remember that, as a kid, I had wanted to be sturdy, like a pillar standing in the rain.

D riving on the freeway, a bus passed me. It was this amazing shade of green. It looked like a true color. My exit was coming up, but I decided to follow the bus. It got off three exits later.

At the top of the incline of the off ramp, traffic stopped for a light. Walking past me up the hill, a man with long hair held a sword like a page from a book. That blew me away. Near the bottom of the hill, a homeless man in ancient-looking clothes held a sign that read, *Stranded*. It felt as though a river was flowing down that hill — and I was flowing with it, convinced an ancient battle had been fought in that valley.

Suddenly, I was Alice floating down the canal — way, way down, having conversations with animals floating alongside her. My life became a book, but "what good are books without conversations?" I flowed down the river to the homeless man so we could have a conversation. More than money, this was the key to staying afloat. I needed to have conversations with God.

I realized I was flowing down the stream to my Wonderland, a journey to be described in the book of my life, *Andy in Wonderland*. And I wondered, how could I have been so quiet in the past, when now I could have conversations — with God and all those He put in my path?

The most powerful thing a person possesses is his testimony. I can testify that there has never been a more broken, defeated and undeserving person who God found and brought out into life than me. Before God pulled me out of that imaginary river, I had never sought His help. There were so many times when I should have.

When I was younger, my car got a flat tire. Fixing things has never been my strong point. I stay away from manly conversations about tools because I know nothing about them. This time, I decided I would change the tire myself. I jacked up the car and began to take the lug nuts off with a giant wrench. It didn't work. Finally, I called Triple A. The mechanic came out and saw me still struggling with the lug nut. "You can't have the car on a jack and the wheel in the air, and get the lug nuts off," he told me. "The tire will just spin."

My struggle for half an hour had been pointless. That summed up my life to that point.

I really connected with music and art from England. *Victoria* by the Kinks was my anthem. This connection made me feel victorious, sure it would lead to great things. Of course, it never made me famous. I identified with Emily Dickinson and her "letter to the world that never wrote to me." Except my letter also added, *P.S.: Thanks for that.*

I also connected with another song by The Kinks, *Dedicated Follower of Fashion,* where a traditional English voice says, "He's a dedicated follower of fashion." I strived not to be that, believing fashion should express something more than "Don't I look good?" Ideas get conveyed by the way we dress. I wanted to say something meaningful through my wardrobe, but didn't know what that something was. I wore a *Happy St. Patrick's Day!* shirt all the time and thought it was funny, I didn't really know what it meant.

England was a different dimension for me. Once, when I was substituting, a teacher asked her assistant to take some large pieces of paper and cut them in half with a paper cutter. But she didn't say that. Instead, she said, "Take these downstairs and give them the business." This inspired me to write a story set in England, using outdated slang. (I owned an outdated slang book from the '70s.) My main character was a young man who didn't go for the latest clothing styles and didn't speak the latest slang. My hero!

Problem was, I wasn't British. Victoria was not my Queen. However inspired by England, its art and music, I might have been. "Mother England," as I called it, wasn't my mother.

Maybe she was a distant aunt.

Thinking of our Founding Fathers coming from England, I always wondered if "Jaywalking" had something to do with John Jay, one of the authors of *The Federalist Papers*. He was a lawyer, after all. I imagined him saying, "Ye may push thy cart across thy road at any angle without anyone bothering thee." In reflection, my future in historical linguistics didn't look so promising. I'd have to find another way to become famous.

To attain fame, I knew I had to be "super keen, " whether I was from England or the United States. I liked the book *1984*, by George Orwell, but saw room for improvement. Instead of "The Two Minute Hate," when citizens of this twisted society would watch videos of the enemy and scream at the screen, my version would include "The Three-Minute Dislike," where citizen would be shown someone eating dinner with a salad fork but keeping his elbows on the table. Finally someone would shout, "That's not very pleasant at all!"

In a similar approach, I included a letter in my story about a character who worried about being put into a room to be tortured until he lost his soul:

> Dear William,
>   This is your soul speaking. I have never been to this world. I know—I should get off my ass and just do it. And because I've never been to this world, it's quite impossible for me to go into Room 42. I know I'm a flake, no need to tell me.
>   Tootles,
>   Bill

48

England – the place my childhood dreams played out, whether it was *Mary Poppins* or *Charlie and The Chocolate Factory*. There were *Bedknobs and Broomsticks*. The language in *My Fair Lady* that was "loverly." I wanted to be part of "this Earth, this realm, this England." But I wasn't a part of it. I needed to "Mobilize My Axioms." as William F. Buckley reportedly said, claiming this slogan would find its way onto every bumper sticker in the world. So, I needed to get started.

Like Buckley, I wanted to be super witty and original. In *Braveheart*, William Wallace states, "It's our wits that make us men." I misinterpreted what that meant. I thought to be witty meant you had to have something hilarious to say every time you opened your mouth. That notion strayed far from the core of *Braveheart*.

My approach was fake and dishonest, to the point of being silly. I tried to be like a Zen Master, answering any question with cryptic wisdom, like, "In Tibet, I wore a robe that weighed seven pounds." No one, including me, knew what that meant, but it still gave me an advantage. Or so I thought.

Being witty would mean I was bigger than any situation I faced. When Zen Masters ponder the problem of how to get a goose out of a bottle without breaking the glass, they simply state, "The goose is out of the bottle." So call me goose boy! Hear me mumble things not even I understand during conversations with myself that make the impossible even more difficult!

I wanted to own original ideas. But only God is an original. Even writing this memoir, being the only one who knows my pain as a Substitute Teacher, I couldn't be truly original.

A friend and fellow poet named George, wrote a Substitute Teacher story about how "If I were a dog I'd be a Chihuahua." I wrote my journey as a Substitute Teacher before I met George. In fact, only recently did I learn from another friend (Lisa, also a teacher) that George had written his story long ago. I had never read George's story, so I couldn't have been thinking of his writing when I wrote a Chihuahua into mine.

Not being completely original doesn't scare me anymore.
Neither do Chihuahuas.

When I see someone with a similar idea, it confirms that my idea is part of a greater web of truth.

I used to worry that I was not the first one to use the word *The* in a title. Others who wrote books, like *The Scarlett Letter* and *The Cat in the Hat*, must have been thinking of me when they added *The* to their titles, because I had the idea of using *The* first. Then I discovered those two books had been written before I was born.

So I still needed a game changer, like *Chuck E. Cheese* did when a rat became the mascot of a nationwide chain of restaurants. Counter-intuitive. I needed to turn things on their heads, defy expectations. How could I be original and still connect with everyone? How could I be popular? That was still a Junior High dream, which fit my Junior High maturity level.

The term "cool" has survived from the middle of the last century. Gangs in *West Side Story* used it during their dance-and-fight, and kids today still use it. Ask a kid how he's are doing, you won't hear him say, "Nifty, Daddy-O," but he might say, "Cool." I think the term "cool" survived because it's a strong delusion. It suggests that kids can be bad, even evil itself.

To be evil is tempting. Parents and society do kids a disservice by giving them credit for being bad. The temptation of thinking you possess evil power was strong for me. It was a hook and lure I bit on and swam with.

I had dedicated my life to be accepted by the "cool" kids. I would invite myself to places they went. In High School, I would call to ask if I could ride in the back of their flat bed pick-up truck on Friday nights. I got to do that for a couple of months, but those nights never led anywhere. Everyone else rode in the cab of the truck. Once, when we stopped to talk to some other guys, someone did the math to figure out how many of us rode in the truck and asked, "Who rides in the back?" And I was, like, "Me!"

Kids are trained from when they are young that they are good when they do this or that. Then they reach an age where it is no longer revered to be good. And I think many kids make the decision "If I can't be good, I will be bad. At least I *am* something." That's how it was with me.

I rebelled without fully understanding what I was rebelling against. I thought my target might be a corrupt system. I bought *Teen Steam Magazine* as a joke — but I also felt that these boy bands might be the problem.

I wrote silly things all over my room, like *Menudo Rules*. Instead of writing *K.I.T.* (Keep In Touch) or *Have a rad summer* in yearbooks, I'd write long diatribes about why Menudo ruled and how the New Kids on the Block had harmony. These were jokes, but I hated these bands. My problem with authority prevented me from asking for help, yet I had no idea how to get anywhere myself.

So many people tried to guide me, but I clung to my knack for getting lost.

The Nest held me for a long time. Collages and pictures hung in the room I nested in. In a poem (*The Nest*), I wondered,

What if you aren't falling?
You have only left your nest
and before you hit the ground,
you fly parallel to the ground
then up out of the canyon
and into the sky.

Music played a huge part in my life back in my days in The Nest. I saw music as being about dissonance. I listened to punk rock to relax. I felt the calmest when listening to the music with the most fight in it.

I overheard someone say, "This town doesn't have the fight in it that other towns have." So I invented Stalemate as a name for a band and waited for someone to ask, "Where are you going tonight?" I had my response ready:

"We're going to see Stalemate down at The Ancient Fence Post."

Music acted as my ultimate pacifier. I reached a point in high school where I preferred being at home, in the dark, in my room, to the discomfort of my life. That's how it was with music.

When I was with friends, I longed for solitude. When I was in solitude, I longed to be with friends. Driving alone in my car became my darkness: my cocoon. It felt like an extension of The Nest.

Darkness is light in refinement. Back then, I made CDs for people. I gave the CDs crazy titles, like *The Woodcutter's Daughter versus Firehose: an all out battle, an ax against a hose*. My brother told me he liked that CD, but that he couldn't tell what songs were on it until he played it.

He was right. I look at those CDs now and have no idea what's on any of them. At the time, they felt so important. They were true to me then. Now I laugh when I read those titles: *Nightfall: A Study in Moppishness*. "Say what?"

Not many friends listened to those CDs. It got to feel like a waste of time. But for truth, no amount is ever wasted, while for Illusion, one penny's worth of time is too much. A couple of CDs out of the hundreds I made still sound inspired. God was using them in my life as true music, helping me get away from dangerous situations in a way that fake music could never do.

In his two million-word journal, Henry David Thoreau asks what kind of scientific examination "enriches the understanding but robs the imagination?"

The artist doesn't explain. The artist shares. I used to explain everything – I called it "pointing," for pointing out things – because I was sure I had *impeccable taste*: "Oh, you like corn muffins? Then you really are the best."

On one radio station I listened to all the time, people would call in to recommend songs to the DJ. It was such a vanity affair:

"Oh, you like that song?" the DJ would say. "Amazing! How did you know it was a good song?"

The caller usually said something like, "I just knew."

My exploitation of music centered on a relationship with God. His Spirit moved through the music and offered help. But I struggled with sharing and couldn't stop pointing, because of my *impeccable taste*. After all, wasn't I the one picking the songs for those CDs?

I had become, almost exclusively, a fulltime pointer.

I gloried in how awesome my taste was. This wasn't true, and all that pointing deeply troubled me, affecting me spiritually. Finally, I made a CD of old and alternative country songs: *A Pointer's Tribute to Country*.

But no song, no artist, no person or thing, can be greater than another. God made all and moves through all — and He can't be greater than Himself. God is God. Comparisons should end there. A list of the greatest Country Music songs ever, as I was trying to do by pointing to them on the CD, was an illusion.

In the movie *High Fidelity*, John Cusack (the only actor whose best film was a teen movie, *Better Off Dead*, made before he got famous), owns a record store. He and an employee (Jack Black) argue about which one of their lists of greatest songs was the best. "My list has German songs on it," Cusack says. That settled it – his list won. *Say what?*

On sports radio, whenever hosts have nothing to talk about (which is quite often), they compare athletes from different eras to determine who was the greatest of all time. The feats of those athletes are moments we become a part of and they are bigger than us, precisely because God is bigger than us. I had to grow into humility.

I wasn't growing to a stage where I didn't need God, just the opposite. I was growing to where I could recognize that I needed God for every breath. I was growing to a level where I could acknowledge that I needed God to take my place and carry me the rest of the way.

The path to becoming a man is a slow one. I remember a Soundgarden song from many years ago: "Slow and steady wins the race but no, that's no way to go." I now believe that's the only way to go.

A cartoon in a recent edition of *The Economist* agreed with me on this. It also made me laugh. At a Moderates Rally, a man with a bullhorn called out to the crowd: "What do we want?" The crowd answered, "Gradual Change!" From the bullhorn: "And when do we want it?" From the crowd: "In due course!"

I had took every shortcut I ever met. They were just detours that slowed down my journey. I thought I was way too wise, that I saw things no one else did, that I could point out things and make them change. I even tried walking in the park blindfolded to test if I could avoid obstacles like benches and trees, and dangers, like lakes and ravines.

I did avoid some of them.

Once, I made out the feet of a woman through a gap at the bottom of my blindfold. I didn't need to see her face to know what she was thinking: "What exactly is that man doing?" And I could feel her chuckle without hearing it.

I also tried wearing sunglasses all the time, indoors and out, so no one could see my eyes. That allowed me to imagine being in another world once I closed my eyes — and no one would never know. I bumped into a lot of things this way, too.

By constantly trying to outthink the world, I ended up outthinking myself. I wanted to be a teacher, but saw myself sitting in a corner of my mind with a dunce cap on, and knowing I deserved the derisive laughter coming my way. Trapped in a foolish time, I knew I was going against God.

This made my struggles as a Substitute Teacher worse, because I knew I deserved what I was getting. So I didn't fight back by writing down names or giving out detention. I had taken a beating my whole life, and came to realize the hard treatment would continue, because I kept taking shortcuts into the viper forest.

G riping and boasting are forever friends. I griped about a lot of things and how difficult they were. The more I whined about how tough my life was, the more I would find myself boasting about how strong I was. I kept putting down God so I could lift myself up.

I had only one way to go: down from the fake pedestal I had put myself on. And there would be no easy way off that pedestal.

I kept repeating this cycle because I still believed I had to make it on my own, without the help of God. I was angry at God for not making me strong enough to succeed without Him. I was never designed to survive that way. So I would climb up my self-made cliff, then fall – over and over, until the day I stopped being angry that I needed to come to God for help. That day, I felt happy because I was finally where I had wanted to be all along.

In my story, *Tram Law: The Musical*, corporations are taking over America. (*Tram Law* is *Wal Mart* spelled backwards.) It resembled *The Simpsons*, when the bullies write things using their fingers against the fogged-up store freezer.

"Some ice cream dude is going to see this and it's gonna blow his mind," one of the bullies says.

All corporations in my story were real ones with their names spelled backwards, like SKCUBRATS. This was one of the most forced stories I ever wrote. But that's how it would usually go back then: God would move and give me a story, then I would think I got the message and I'd write a garbage ode — a celebration of garbage.

It's the same thing with bands. They write 10 crap songs, then God gives them a good one and they tell the interviewer, "We've been writing music for a long time. This is one of the many great songs we've come up with." God blesses them in the beginning, but when they don't give God the glory, He won't bless them again until they do. It would actually hurt them more to bless them when they can't handle fame. Only God can handle glory. This explains why, when asked, "Do you like that band?" a fan might say, "I like their old stuff."

Another explanation might be it was time to do something else. We're not meant to do only one thing. We invest our talents to make new ones, and in the process, we are humbled.

No one is called to be great guitarist, just a humble actor on a stage, pulling the string of their Teddy Ruxpin doll, doing a dance of shame. Many talented musicians fall into that trap. They hold on to their self-image as a great guitarist or singer or drummer. On tour, they play their old stuff to crowds. They should be working to develop other talents. We all should. Even a great guitarist stops playing at his best level at some point.

And while in our prime, we can still mess up, especially when we think we know everything. Sports announcers and pundits make this mistake all the time. Before a game, they'll predict one team will dominate the other. The game starts, their team starts losing. "This is an entirely different team. They don't make mistakes like this."

Sure they do. And the sports pundit doesn't want to admit he didn't see it coming. He put all of his stock into a vessel, but none into God, who is using the vessels.

Few people with big egos want to admit a higher power might be responsible for their success. I remember one announcer talking about how luck always plays a part. His broadcasting partner disagreed: "Luck has nothing to do with it." I don't believe in luck, but outside forces, especially a higher power, have everything to do with it.

Why do we believe the predictions of sports pundits, then forget all about that the next day when those predictions proved wrong? Then, the next week, we go back to believing their predictions again. It all comes down us, not the predictors. We don't want to admit we were wrong, or foolish enough to believe someone who was wrong.

When we vote for a politician who loses, part of us wants to see the candidate who got elected fail. Why? Because we didn't vote for him, and we don't want to be wrong.

This is how I was living my life.

projected my philosophies onto the world. I was sexist, believing that all women had the same taste, so if I could impress one, I would impress them all. This led to my being rejected. A lot. And I enjoyed rejecting women to get back at all of them. Then I learned that there is no universal appeal. Each woman is an individual. The answer isn't in a short article in *People Magazine.*

In a story I wrote on this realization, the main character gives a valedictory speech at his graduation, claiming that *Cosmopolitan* and other magazines like it are a scam. The Editor of *Cosmopolitan* appears out of nowhere, runs on stage and announces, "Don't worry Class of 2019, your Valedictorian is lying. And in 1998, Harrison Ford was the Sexiest Man Alive."

A sigh of relief goes through the crowd.

Thinking I had it all figured out, I wasted my nights trying to "get lucky" and go home with someone. Now I spend my nights trying *not* to go home with someone. So, basically, I'm getting the same results.

The world is "deceiving and being deceived" – 2 Timothy 3:13. There is so much waiting for nothing. Ads hype a great lifestyle, one full of promise. This promise, that sales pitch, is a lie. That lifestyle never led me anywhere. Pride had me thinking that waiting for nothing would all pay off someday. I was my problem.

was a wanna-be pretty boy. The only problem was, I wasn't very pretty. Even if I did get a girl to look at me, I froze, thinking, "Now what?"

I never found a way to talk to women. And the body follows the spirit. The spirit doesn't follow the body, no matter how many push-ups you do or how much hair gel you use. I found myself in a quagmire of clothing colors. But I was about to discover the best and the worst thing about women:

If you don't talk to women, they pretty much leave you alone.

I practiced a lot of facial expressions. I grew a goatee to make me look suave and worldly. And I wouldn't smile – that wouldn't look good with a goatee. So, I was miserable.

I couldn't smile. But I looked cool, right? And every place I went, I'd make all these facial expressions. For reasons I couldn't figure out back then, none of this attracted ladies. Then a friend of my brother said, "Andy, you look like you want to tear somebody's head off."

All this time, I thought I looked tender, attractive, alluring. I remember staring at myself in the mirror, wondering where I had gone wrong.

T he problem with mirrors is, good or bad, what you see is not you.

I would lock myself in the bathroom and tell my reflection, "I'm not leaving this room until I make myself perfect — facial expressions and body." But my mirror didn't work. It couldn't make this happen.

A new mirror wouldn't do the trick. I tried to make myself perfect in every mirror I encountered. Same results.

I wrote about women back then: "I know you think I'm in love with you and I want to shower you with wealth, but it's not true. I'm really in love with myself."

That's where the mirrors led me. They were a bitter river, showing me my face. And I grew bitter about that.

I n my dream, I'm a toy in a room with other toys. Our bodies are covered in Lego-like pieces. Another toy uses a megaphone to tell us, "Remove your Ken and Barbie accessories. Rip them off! You can't dress like a toy and expect to be treated like a person. Join the Moppet Rebellion!"

Then a light goes on in the hallway and all the toys yell, "Andy's coming! Everybody hide!"

T he cavern I had built for myself kept me hidden. I thought that if I wore sunglasses and a hat, no one could see me. But people see you no matter how many layers of clothes you wear. That's where those facial expressions came in.

I truly felt I could control any situation with my practiced facial expressions. I had different looks, each with a different kind of power and effect.

At a restaurant I liked, a guitarist played so quietly we called him "The Sponge." His music cancelled out room noise. He seemed to absorb the rattling of glasses, the clink of silverware hitting plates. The Sponge had a negative amount of sound coming out of his guitar. That's how I wanted to be.

I wanted to hide and not make any ripples in the water. But I was as successful as that key-hiding magnet, the one with those big letters that spelled *Hide-A-Key*. No pair of sunglasses or type of hat could make me invisible because it wasn't up to me. I was the "me-est me there ever was," as Steve Martin once said. And I wasn't going anywhere anytime soon.

The Devil's game is the only game you lose just by playing it. I had already lost, but not only did I think I could still win, I thought I was going to be like King Puma in the Pro Wrestling Nintendo video game. No one could pin him. The only way to win was to throw him out of the ring and make him be counted out (20 seconds and you're out).

But what kind of victory was that? Deep down, every player knew he couldn't defeat King Puma, who laughed as the referee raised your arm. That laugh told me this was false victory.

Back then, I wanted to be my body and not me the person, because I knew I could improve my body. As a person, you can't do anything or make anyone else feel anything without God.

I thought the Devil's Flattery was success. Watching the scene in *Creepshow* where a high school kid gets sucked through a floating dock and his ring comes off between the boards, I blurted out, "He won the High School Trophy!" I thought this kind of spontaneous comment showed my quick wit and deep understanding.

All it really showed was that God was using my fake years to mold me into something real.

I have always felt watched by the watch men.
My face has been less an instrument to express my feelings than a tool to convince others that I felt anything at all.

I took a quiz for a sales job. Question 1: *Do you feel everyone is watching you when you go down the street?*

Question 2: *Do you regularly apologize for existing?*

I answered *No* to each question, recognizing that's what the bosses wanted to hear. Both were absolute lies.

I felt I was putting on a show my whole life – trying to give the best performance anyone had ever seen, convincing others that I was really a person. I didn't believe I was one. This became a major problem. I couldn't have meaningful relationships because, I was always acting, even with people I was close to.

I got that sales job — the one with the questions about being watched and regular apologizing? My boss told me, "You're a terrible salesman, but you shouldn't be. You got 100% on the quiz. That's why we hired you!"

I didn't sell a thing the whole time I worked there,

I should have checked my watch, if I had owned one, because the time had come for me to find a new job to fail at.

I knew I could do it.

THE WANDERER

THE JOB COACH
YEARS

I threw a boomerang that never came back.

— Anonymous

1

After living with my parents for a while, I moved back to San Diego to become a Job Coach, mentoring disabled adults at their places of work. My job required me to make sure they did their jobs right, then I would talk to their supervisors to make sure all was going well. In reality, as a Job Coach, my main job was to stand there.

Sometimes I had to watch someone bag groceries for eight hours. There was absolutely nothing to think about, which was right up my alley. As a character on *Parks and Recreation* says while licking hundreds of envelopes, "This work makes sense to me."

Could my mind have gone somewhere if it had wanted to? Sure, but where? To *Carolina in My Mind*? But I felt content right where I was, watching. Others could ask me the simplest question and I wouldn't know the answer. I might have looked as though I was in a food coma kind of state, but I was happy where I was, taking stock of the opportunities around me.

At the end of the check stand: a DVD on sale with *Cloudy with a Chance of Meatballs* One and Two on it. The Cloudy Collection!

I saw that generic items had come a long way since a bottle of beer was simply called *beer* on its white label. Now, cereal aisles had *Silly Circles*. *Mountain Lightning* sat next to *Dr. Skipper* in the soda aisle. My eyes were being opened to a new generic reality as I watched my clients stock shelves, place security tags on items. Did I mention that obsessive thoughts could recur?

And the music in these grocery stores drove me crazy: Musak versions of boy band songs that I had made fun of in Junior High. Worse yet, the actual versions of those same songs also got played. It was as if I was being punished by the photos of bands I used to put on the walls of my room in Junior High as a joke. I had *Teen Beat Magazines* with Menudo and The New Kids on the Block. And now they were singing in the halls of my mind as well as in the aisles of the store. They tormented me with angry remarks: "You made fun of my hair." *The Revenge of Richard Marx.*

I kept trying to avoid boredom. Ironically, thinking a lot withers the mind, while boredom and downtime preserve it. My whole life had been downtime, so being a Job Coach sent my mind into uptime.

Stuck in traffic, I'd think, "I'm going to think and solve problems in my life and when the traffic stops, I will stop thinking and be farther along than when I started this drive." The traffic stopped. My mind didn't.

It felt as though I had started my wheels spinning and the train conductor had fallen asleep and the train's brakes were out: next stop – Brick Wall. If anyone asked, I could tell them, "Brick Wall is lovely this time of year. I spent my early job-coaching career in Brick Wall."

In college, I read a commentary on T.S. Eliot's *Waste Land*, describing the poem as being about a time when we are too conscious. That was me as a Job Coach in those early days. My shadow would follow me with this killer consciousness, urging me to imagine scenarios to keep myself sane.

One time, in a grocery store, I spotted a kid's race car shopping cart, complete with a steering wheel. Nearby: a police car cart. I pictured the racer cart speeding down the frozen food aisle, the cop cart in close pursuit. The kid in the racer checked his rearview mirror and said, "I'm getting blown up again? This is my second ticket in two weeks!"

At the checkout lane, the police cart parked behind the racer, whose driver turned and said, "Yeah, I've got my license and registration. You know that was a speed trap don't you? The frozen food aisle had water on the ground, I couldn't slow down."

The kid in the police cart wore sunglasses. He nodded and gave the racer a ticket.

While my mind was still lost at this point, my heart was beginning to be found. I stopped recreational drug use, including alcohol, as I had a problem with that, and realized that I empathized with the individuals I was job-coaching because they had hearts of love. They wanted to teach me to know love in the same way that they did. They seemed to know that I needed to learn.

Technically, then, I was the one being coached. That was fine with me – I was used to not being in charge. It became clear that I was where I needed to be. I was home. The Chihuahua had come back as the new sheriff in town and my badge – dog tag – was shiny.

Like the wizard floating above Oz in his hot air balloon, I explored space in the netherdome. The sky was a circus tent with its roof hanging down as I ran into the madras and silk. And there were clouds of cotton. I now had a ship to stay afloat above the sky.

As a Job Coach, I was not allowed to read a book. Or check my cell phone. Or help the clients with their work. I still remember my friend saying in amazement, "Let me get this straight. You're not allowed to work?"

Some people might be envious, but I had things to keep me busy, usually. Still, the stars do line up sometimes when my clients knew what they were doing and I just had to stand there and watch.

As they bagged groceries, I gazed into the abyss beneath the piñatas hanging from the ceiling above the checkout registers: *SpongeBob* smiled down at me. This would be the only job I knew of where I got in trouble for working. "What did you get fired for?" a friend asked.

I could only sigh. "Working extra hard."

Often, I job-coached in a kitchen, watching clients wash dishes. I felt so in the way, no matter where I stood. And I felt as though everyone was wondering, "What are you doing here exactly?" But God was always moving. Some kitchen workers felt sorry for me: "Hey Mac, what did you get in trouble for again?"

"Working."

"It's tough all over. Hey, Susie, make my pal here a bowl of red noise – on me."

I had learned the phrase *red noise* from a book of out-of-date slang from the '70s. It meant tomato soup. I ate a lot of soup while my clients benefitted from my just being there.

Some kitchen employees thought I was the Health Inspector, so they worked extra carefully around me. Customers in grocery stores usually thought I was the Manager, because I wore a dress shirt. They'd come up to me to complain, or tell me how much they liked that store. I'd just nod. Some people went on and on about a project they were doing at their house, then they'd suddenly ask me, "Do you carry Spicy Brown Mustard?"

All I could do is tell them, "I don't know," and watch them move on to ask someone else.

On a military base, I was Job Coach-in-Charge of a small group within a bigger group of workers. Our work leader spoke Spanish. She referred to my position as a "Mimis" – baby sleeping, a loving way of saying, "night-night." She gave out assignments that way: William – vacuum, Tristam – sweeping, Andy – mimis.

Many of my clients started as entry level courtesy clerks in grocery stores, so they had to watch training videos, like *Smile, Greet and Take the Customer to the Item*. Nothing wrong with that, but these videos urged fake behavior. They reminded me of going to a favorite frozen yogurt store and being asked, "Would you like to be part of the Smileage Club?" One time, I asked a team member there how her day was going. She smiled and said, "Grand."

One Manager at a grocery store told me, "Those videos are scary." My clients would never respond to a question like "How are you?" with a "Splendid!" or "Grand!" And they didn't have to. They were genuine. Customers appreciated that. They loved my clients and showered them with compliments: "They gave the sweetest customer service." Those "Grand" employees never received that kind of grateful response.

Divine providence must have set the teaching credential program GPA requirement at 2.7. I graduated college with a 2.6. Both times I applied for a credential, they rejected me. The first time, I tried to fill out the application with what I thought they wanted to hear. The second time, told them what I really felt. I was genuine. I received a genuine rejection.

And I felt elated. Teaching clearly wasn't the job for me. I had decided well before this that I should try odd jobs—that was how I would grow. Job Coaching became the oddest job of all.

It was a job without walls or boundaries, a job that forced me to learn how to fly and not depend on everyone else to tell me what to do. It was like me—undefined.

People would ask me all the time who I was and what I was doing there. I asked myself the same questions.

One of the first times I Job-Coached, at a movie theater, I worked for my scheduled hour, then walked to the parking lot thinking, *I am really organized now*. I dug into a pocket, then another, unable to find my car keys. My car was unlocked. I felt relief, then glanced at the ignition. *Found the keys!* And the car was still running!

I hadn't burned up too much gas, and the air conditioner still worked – my car had never felt this refrigerator cold before – so I drove away, congratulating myself.

I used to flip my flip phone in the air and catch it just to keep my hands busy. I believed I could perfect the art of never failing to catch it, even when looking the other way. The battery popped out of that phone every time it hit the ground – hundreds of times.

In the movies, the hero punches a punching bag for a short time while inspirational music plays in the background. Suddenly, he has become perfect. He can't lose. I was finding out with my flip phone experiment that losing was an option.

We can't make ourselves perfect when we were all created imperfect. But I kept trying, blaming the world for being imperfect, so it couldn't be my fault.

My phone's battery came out so often, it stopped working. I replaced it with a touch screen model. I missed opening, then spinning my flip phone on a table helicopter-rotor fast, something people couldn't do with their smart phones. I even missed dropping it.

I didn't miss being a Substitute Teacher. I was too spacey to be effective. Once, a group of High Schoolers left my class for an assembly. Five minutes later, they came back with Jack in The Box and started eating it at their desks. I watched them chew, thinking, "Now that shouldn't be."

My "trippy" approach in the classroom didn't go over well with parents or other teachers. I had been crippled by my own behavior to act on dealing with the behavior of students, reducing my role to that of a casual observer.

As a Job Coach, I felt I was moving in the right direction. On a biking trip in Utah, my friend's mom's boyfriend asked me if I knew how to back a trailer up. I said, "Sure," got in his truck and backed up into the trailer, jack-knifing it. The more gas I gave the situation, the more sideways the trailer got, until the truck's wheel were spinning, going nowhere. The truck owner took it from there.

Later that same day, I drove the truck, this time without the trailer. Over rocky terrain, I must have used the wrong gear and got stuck. This time the smell coming from the engine worried me, and there was dust everywhere. The truck's owner came up to driver's window again and said, very calmly, "My clutch is on fire."

Even though I had no idea how I had arrived in this moment or what would happen next, I remember feeling that I was getting help. I had a guide.

On U2's first album, Bono sings: "Into the heart of child, I stay a while. I can go there."

The imagination refreshes. This is rest – downtime. It's a good thing. There is a time and place for Facebook and social media, but these offer no spiritual refuge. God is not a dot-com. When we reach the point where we are typing "help" into our I Phones – instead of praying to God – there is an issue.

The internet can be useful finding help in times of crisis, but Siri is not God. Try asking Siri an unsolvable problem and you might get a response about Cookie Monster having no cookies and you having no friends. "But Siri, I thought *we* were friends!"

A recent Facebook post made me laugh: "Just saw a guy at Starbucks. He wasn't on a tablet or looking at his cell phone. He was just sitting there. What a psychopath." These days, if we're not connected to the internet, we are exhibiting suspicious behavior.

There were few cell phones in use when I began Substitute Teaching. Land lines were normal back then. I didn't have internet access on my flip phone when I started as a Job Coach. Now, when I'm bored, I check my I phone. It's a knee-jerk reaction. I check my emails an uncountable number of times a day. Facebook, too. I thought about going back to a flip phone just to stop the madness. Since I am not supposed to use my phone at work, anyway, I fight the insanity of boredom with a device that encourages insanity. I am fighting fire with Firefox. I'm what I smell burning now.

Today we use cell phones to hide. I know I do. Everyday conversations happen less frequently for me because the discomfort that usually causes conversations isn't there – I'm looking at my cell phone! – so I begin a silent conversation with myself:

I would be uncomfortable, I just got so busy farming on Farmville. And I'm in a band on Yoville. (I don't like to brag but I just got 15 likes.) It's nothing major, I just keep living my life on that humble path, you know?

The technology of wireless connections is dazzling. While driving in my car, a friend was arguing with his girlfriend on the phone. I didn't know he even had a girlfriend. "Having some problems with her?" I asked.

"Yeah," he said, "we've broken up seven times."

I kept my eyes on the road. "I could drop you off at her place."

"She lives in Las Vegas. We've never met."

An ad for a cable company described an employee of a competitor answering the phone with, "Intergalactic Cable." Cable hadn't come to my hometown when I was a kid. When I first lived in the Old Town area of San Diego, getting cable meant paying for every aspect of installation, including underground burial of the cable. One notice I got read, "We will be able to offer you our cable services for $14,000."

The Coleco technology I enjoyed as a kid produced a hand-held football game with only lights that lit up, no video images. This technology was still being used for the Chargers' scoreboard before they moved to Los Angeles in 2016. My brother and I would wonder if fans were going to play *Pong* on that scoreboard at halftime.

I liked playing that old hand-held football game and having to imagine the players. Chargers Stadium scoreboard did have a small video screen, so that required fans to use a lot of imagination, too.

Kids used imagination so much that imagination became how kids viewed who they were. That's how it should be at that age. At some point, adults have to believe their own eyes. But being led through life only by your eyes is like Rocky Balboa leading in the ring with his face. You get pounded so badly that eventually you have to tell your your manager, "Cut me Mick. Cut me."

That's no way to box. Or to live.

My problem with cell phones? Too much input. It's like "Feed Bags" on *Saturday Night Live*. Strap on a breakfast bag and eat it on the way to work. Sometimes you choke.

That sums up cell phones for me: internet, Facebook, emails all the time. God would do something great for me, but instead of appreciating it, taking time to enjoy it and be grateful, I got busy with the next Facebook thing. It felt like not digesting my food after eating. With enough trivial videos to make me puke, I got very little nutrition.

Small moves are the only way life works for me now. If I walk a couple of blocks and take a break, life is a gift. But I had lived my life as an uninterrupted trek. While in Manhattan to visit a cousin, I got off the train with a duffle as big as a body bag: five feet long. Packed, it weighed over 60 pounds. I carried it 30 blocks without a break.

My cousin stared in disbelief. "You carried that thing through the city?"

In that instant, I remembered bumping in to people on the street, getting dirty looks. I had carried that monstrosity of a duffle into a movie theater to watch *War of the Worlds*. Good thing there were lots of empty seats.

I didn't realize then that I was responsible for the excess input in my life. I was my own cell phone, the person choking on the feed bag, desperate to make it the full 30 blocks without a break.

B ack when few people had cell phones, I took my niece and her friend to a football game. Both girls were about five years old. My niece's friend had a cell phone and she talked about nothing on that phone the entire game. Her nonsensical conversation foreshadowed how my life would be affected by cell phones—not much to say, but input, more input, even more input, you scream your output: "Siri! Help!"

Years later, my niece texted her friend who was sitting next to her. *Stop The Madness* remains the mantra of my generation. It's not just an Aerobics video anymore!

A moonship lands on the water. By a wind-kissed willow tree, I hold a lantern. An alien horn sounds in the distance. Water dribbles out in rings on the surface. Like a song that springs from silence, the ship from an alien land has come at night to creep into our days and silence our minds.

THE THOUGHTLESS ONE

In high school, my class chose me *Biggest Air Head*. When the photographer came to take my picture, I was too proud and shot an angry look into the camera, so that photo never made it into the yearbook.

I also earned a *Granite* award in football – not because I played like one of the Seven Blocks of Granite from Notre Dame football lore, but because I was a granite blockhead.

Back then, part of me actually believed these awards carried virtue: *The Tao of Pooh* or *The Tao of Drew*.

Achieving thoughtlessness would lead me to another level. I expressed my frustration by writing, *I wanted to be a Taoist but couldn't live like a piece of wood.*

Of course, I still had my achievements: *Biggest Air Head* award, *Granite* award, fired from two bus boy jobs. I got fired from the first one for throwing away silverware (it had been wrapped in the napkins) and from the second for being too slow. I told those truths on a job application:

Experience – Bus Boy

Reason For Leaving Job – fired (lost silverware; too slow).

The truth didn't help me much.

Blockheadedness – if I could call it that (a blockhead makes up all sorts of words) – is an art form. As a kid, looking at a rack of seedless grapes, I wondered "How did they get the seeds out?" An honest inquiry, similar to when a friend stared at a grove of orange trees and said, "Why don't those oranges have stickers on them, like at the store?"

Childlike curiosity can come before a mental breakthrough. As a pizza delivery guy, I thought I was smarter than the guys I worked with because I was writing stories. I couldn't stop spouting blockhead lines:

"Swords aren't sharp. They can't hurt you"

"Water doesn't make you go to the bathroom. Soda does."

I also set delivery boy records for being lost. Maps weren't much help. My boss called me a comedy of errors. In my mind, I could have been starring in a superhero movie: *Called to be Blockheads.*

INT. BANK – DAY

THEME MUSIC OUT

BLOCK MAN and BLOCK BOY race in to stop a robbery-in-progress. But all is quiet inside.

BLOCK MAN
Is this the right bank?

BLOCK BOY
(checks note in his hand)
It's where the Police Commish
told us to go. (beat) Pretty sure.

It goes downhill from there. They argue. It gets dark, the street lights come on. They're broke, no money for a taxi. Worst superheroes ever.

Is there such thing as intelligence, or only God's guidance? God is the only smart one, so when we mishear our own intentions, we become blockheads. It's out of our control.

The more humbled I got, the less of a blockhead I became.

(Of course, whenever my city needs me, the Blockhead Symbol will shine in the night sky, and this blockhead will have a tear in his eye and remember. . .)

S ays here you worked at our other branch for three years," the manager said, glancing at my job application.

"Yeah, I was there for a while."

That was the restaurant that fired me for tossing out the silverware by mistake.

"We need a good waiter who can handle a lot of tables at once."

"I'm great with numbers," I told him.

We shook hands. He took the *Help Wanted* sign out of the diner window. "Show up tomorrow," he said, "with your server's card."

Never having been a waiter, I had no server's card. I didn't show up. (*Historical note*: years later, I worked as a waiter and got fired for gross incompetence. I was—and am—terrible with numbers.)

A friend told my brother, "After age 30, a writer's brain turns to mush." My brain achieved that faster than normal.

Movie Idea: Writers' brains turning to goo: a horror film. Think—*The Blob*.

B lockheadedness comes out of love. Favorite stories families tell involve what a kid said one time, something so genuine and out of context, it becomes a precious memory:

Mother: "Any homework left to do for tomorrow?"

Daughter: "Just a full-scale model of Jamestown."

My niece had a job at a movie theater and called in sick. Then she went to the theater to see a movie. The boss saw her there and fired her. When I asked her why she would go to that particular theater, the one she worked at, that she had just called in sick to, she said, "I had to. That's the only place I get my employee discount."

B eing a Job Coach is the perfect writer's job. It affords time to focus on good things, like love and the like, and frees your mind to write (or turn to mush) – busy enough not to be a total mush head, but free enough to focus on the miracles God performs.

An obsessive thought might intrude: *Should I submit this poem?* That might drive me crazy, because a Job Coach has very little to think about. Fortunately, my clients kept me in a good place.

I'd get calls from them. Some of those messages were absolute life savers. During obsessive fits of despair, I might get a call from an angel (client) that would pull my heart back to a place where I'm present and focused on the good things going on around me.

For a short time, I was a valet for The Hyatt Regency in downtown San Diego. My own natural ability to get lost helped me see the same ability in others. People I handed car keys to would ask, "Do you know how to get to Balboa Park?"

I'd give them my best guess. Some of us have a map in our heads. I didn't even have a *Speak-And-Spell* in mine. I wasn't trying to get those drivers lost – and maybe I didn't. Maybe each of them found Balboa Park or wherever they were going. After all, I never did see any of those people again.

Baseball slugger Fred McGriff, who tied Lou Gehrig in career home runs, had come to town with the Atlanta Braves to face the San Diego Padres. I got handed his ticket and sent to get his car. I searched for over an hour before finding his keys. As a Padres fan, I hoped I was partially responsible for his being late to the game.

I remember looking at the sky that night as the sun was setting, thinking, *the Padres need me.* I had been called to be a blockhead and I had answered the call.

That one was for the Padres!

A s manager for a friend's band, I went to clubs, gave them the band's CD, and tried to convince club owners to book the band. Once, after telling the owner, "They're a great band," I turned and walked into the wall. *Strike One.*

As I drove off, the CD started playing. It was still in my car CD player. I had given the club owner a blank CD. *Strike Two.*

The band got the gig. *Home Run.*

Band Manager-Booking Agent Extraordinaire, I felt ready to take on the world. From my new vantage point, I could see far into the ocean. I was ready to leave the nest

I stood at wit's end
I would have jumped off
the cliff and tried to fly

But I
couldn't think
of a clever
ending to the
story

2

RISK IS THE

FIT THAT I

HAVE BEEN THROWING

SINCE BIRTH

Just like smart phones make dumb people, I blame TV for my own dumbness. I watched the *Batman* series and I sucked my thumb until late in childhood. My poem, *No Thumbsucking in Eternity*, stressed the need to stop doing the things in everyday life that would keep me from living in Eternity.

I wrote this without knowing any of the laws of Eternity. The only law I learned in childhood came from TV: *The Law Of Raisins: Two Scoops – That's a lot of raisins.* But my poem expressed what I still believe: true art was born in Eternity and it never left.

TV acted as a baby's pacifier for me as a kid. When a commercial interrupted *Conan The Barbarian*, my brother joked, "And Conan wears Jordache Jeans." He nailed it. TV makes us feel that heroes are better than everyone else. Girls ask them out. They use the products we should buy. Pacified by TV, that became my solution. I could suck my thumb my whole life if I could be a hero. *Conan* was sponsored by Jordache Jeans. Someday, they'd sponsor me.

My arrogance made me believe this would be possible. I had to make an effort to throw away all my pacifiers (even though using one, as an adult, is considered hip and avant garde). I can still watch TV and enjoy it, but it is no longer my pacifier.

But maybe one day, Jordache will call to sponsor me.

friend agreed with me: "Everyone believes the scenarios on TV are real." Shows set in offices portray dynamic inter-actions. Everyone has a joke ready for every situation. In real life, we feel pressure to recreate that in our work place. Jerry Seinfeld's stand-up bit about working in an office makes fun of this: "Every time you go to the bathroom and you pass people in the hall, they say, `Tight Quarters,' or `Howdy,' or the barely perceptible `Hey'." He concludes that we should act like Vulcans on *Star Trek* and just say, "Acknowledge."

I used that barely perceptible "Hey." I couldn't figure out if the other person would to say, "Hi" before I did. This reduced me to a half-hearted recluse who talked to no one, especially when I worked on military bases. Should I say, "Sir?" or "Good morning, Sir?" Some got angry: "Don't call me Sir. I work for a living." These kinds of things took over my life. Something so small had such power.

And I would still feel distracted around women, focusing on obsessive thoughts to avoid talking to them.

TV teaches us to have no social boundaries. As a teenager, I walked into a friend's house. His mother said, "You can't just come in without knocking."

It shocked me: "But that's how the Fonz does it on *Happy Days!*"

elevision teaches us to look at people differently. We stare at actors on TV but they that can't see us. In real life, staring at someone would make that person uncomfortable. Nobody likes being gawked at. I even treated my own reflection with that same lack of respect. Pretty soon, I believed my body had powers it could never have. That made me wonder if TV was turning all of us into Peeping Toms.

I fooled myself into thinking I understood the problem with TV: the screen was flat. If that screen were three-dimensional, like real life, the world would change. So to my mind, 3-D TV was a spiritual necessity.

The problem, of course, had nothing to do with the screen. I treated the TV like an idol. I expected it to live for me: I had turned into Homer Simpson, slapping the set and telling it, "Stupid TV. Be more funny."

Baseball looks easy on TV. In Little League, I pitched a couple of games, convinced my fastball had real heat. As a college student, I tried my hand at a carnival booth that timed the speed people threw a baseball. A big guy like me would probably awe the onlookers. Puffed up, I went into my wind up and hurled my best fastball: 60 miles per hour – slow even for a Little Leaguer.

In that moment, it all came back to me. The best hitter in our Little League hit three home runs off me in a single game. The second homer was the hardest hit ball any of us had ever seen. Six feet off the ground, that line drive looked like it was going to go right through a tree. I knew it was gone before I could turn my head to watch it leave the park. His third home run went so far, I couldn't actually see it land.

I would write a story in 8th grade about that game. Instead of feeling like the worst pitcher ever, I felt like a hero – like Michael Jackson singing *We Are The World*. Giving up those three homeruns would give this young athlete confidence, enough to keep him working on his baseball skills and get to the Major Leagues. I wrote that story as a joke. But this guy actually made it to the Majors.

It remains one of my greatest accomplishments.

Bringing my baseball heroics with me to High School, I signed on as a Little League umpire, sure that I had baseball wisdom to impart. In first my game, working the first base line, I thought, "People might suspect I don't what I'm doing. I need to call a balk."

When I did, the manager ran out of dugout to protest. I informed him that his pitcher had not come to a complete stop. Only later would I remember that Little League rules don't require a pitcher to come to a complete stop before delivering the ball to home plate, because Little League runners are not permitted to take a lead off the bases and therefore can't be fooled by pitchers and picked off.

So my first game as an ump got protested.

I quit after five games. I had spent $120 for umpire's equipment. At $20 per game, I lost money. It wasn't the first time.

Or the last.

Minor League Little Leaguers all want to play in the next level up, for a Major League Little League team. The son of a friend plays on a Minor League team called The Storm on a field close to me. An actual Class A Minor League team, also called The Storm, plays an hour north of me in Lake Elsinore, as a San Diego Padres farm club. Do the Minor League Little Leaguers dream of joining the older kids in the Major Leagues of Little League and say things similar to the dialogue in *Bull Durham*?

"When I get to The Show, there's going to be crisp towels and gum the likes of which you've never seen."

"Bubble Gum?"

"Double Bubble."

"Whoa!"

3

HE had already lost
the foosball game but
he got one bonus ball
This one was for pride

The Pride Ball

All things considered, pride kept me the village fool. The first elementary school I substituted at, I finished my interview by telling the Principal, "I'm going to lead the children to new heights of mental engagement with music."

"Great!" she said. "What do you think of Mahler's Fifth?"

"Yes, I agree!" I said, unsure about that symphony or its composer. I kept agreeing with her, then walked to my Kindergarten class. Another teacher had his class lined up outside next to mine. I joked with him, using big words the kids wouldn't understand and feeling so smart, basking in the other teacher's laughter. After the class, he laughed when he told me, "I heard a wall of sound coming from your class and the decibels increased as the children screamed louder."

I had held control of my first class for almost 10 seconds.

An artist I studied in college would write things on billboards – strange statements – then stand beneath the billboard to see how people reacted. In my story *Fillerless Rope*, someone put copies of an article in newspaper racks and on railings throughout town. He would then wait to experience people's reactions.

At a friend's house, where everyone would drink way too much beer, I placed my story where everyone could read it. Later that night, I found the story on the ground, covered in footprints. A similar thing had happened wherever I left the story. People ignored it, leaving it in the newspaper rack or on the railing. But this felt worse. These were my friends. I had finally gotten a reaction. It wasn't what I had been hoping for.

Fortunately, I had friends put in my life by God who were supportive of me and my attempts at writing. Some good advice came in a rejection letter, advising me to read my poems at poetry events. I joined a monthly poetry circle called Full Moon Poets. It turned out to be the single best artistic move I ever made.

A group of poets featuring at one of our meetings – Mother, Maiden, Crone – changed my life. Those three women poets introduced me to the *San Diego Poetry Annual*, which exposed me to a wider web of poets and poems. I started getting confident.

By the time a big Poetry Slam came up, I was sure I'd do great, maybe even win the thing. The thought of that excited me. The crowd's applause would reverse that beer party embarrassment.

This got me thinking about a hip clothing store called *Justice*, with a heart dotting the *i*. I used to laugh at that name, because it sounded like a Metallica album. My brother made fun of that store: "And there can be no justice without affordable teen-ware for girls aged 13-16." Our cousin used to take his daughter shopping at that store. Every time he walked through the door, he'd announce, "I'm seeking Justice!"

If there was any justice in the world, my sheer awesomeness at the Poetry Slam would bring victory my way.

Is this full-contact Poetry?" my brother joked.
Instantly, I imagined clotheslining my competitor poets, like Donald Trump had clotheslined Vince McMahon in the *Battle of the Billionaires* at a World Wrestling Federation event.

"Will you be reading *Basho*?" my brother asked.

I visualized hitting someone with a foreign object, like George *The Animal* Steele had before eating the turnbuckle on *Saturday Morning Wrestling*.

"Steel cage or can you tap out?"

I could put my boot around the ring rope, like Larry Zabisco before he bashed someone with a steel chair.

I got knocked out in the first round of that Poetry Slam, scoring a 2 out of a possible 10. I felt like all those no-named opponents who lost every Saturday Morning—the wrestlers who receive no boos or cheers when their names are announced or when the leave the ring, having never having landed a single blow.

Their names, like mine leaving the stage that night, simply echoed in the arena like noise.

Those reading before me at the Poetry Slam all got 8's. Sometimes the crowd would boo and demand the judges award a 10. When my score of 2 was announced, no one argued against it.

That night at home, I fell down, figuratively and literally. But I chose to trust in and live for the one who had caught me—God.

The crowd's approval no longer seemed important. The desire to be famous dried up. I no longer wanted to be published to prove how awesome I was, but rather, to invest what God had given me for His glory. That score of 2 ended up being OK after all. No need to go to the mythical 11 of *Spinal Tap*.

Dreams of impressing people for approval began to fade. Looking back at my time in a band named Permission — so called because I felt I had permission to do whatever I wanted — I realized I was now giving myself permission to live true to God. Where I had previously been on a field trip with a permission slip taped to my forehead, I was now free to follow God. No hall monitor could stop me.

Just the other day, I spotted a class of 2nd graders led on a field trip by a teacher who held a single string she had tied to each little hand. It reminded me of an episode of *The Simpsons*: a newly invented baby translator gets tested on Maggie, the infant of the family wearing a harness. She says, "This leash demeans us both."

In another episode, Bart Simpson becomes the bully hall monitor. His picked-on classmate Millhouse yells to the kid-packed cafeteria, "Sure we have order, but at what price?" That had summed up my life before this new turning point. I maintained control by carefully stepping in line with what I thought was the world's approval.

It was only when I went into free-fall, landing on my face at the Poetry Slam, that I realized God could fly — and He could catch me and carry me away from all predicaments and adversity I might face.

My stallion was fierce
Then I noticed a stick coming
out of its back and up to the ceiling
and it connected to the floor
Then I realized I was on a carousel
And I was the only one on it
I grabbed for the ring
and got it again and again
I could get a free ride
But, hey, I got on this thing for free anyway
I got down and threw my rings away
and wasn't feeling so merry
Then I saw the name of the ride —
Approval is Slavery

I carried a letter I had just received in the mail out to the deck. A sun-peaked, clouded sky shone over a massive tree. I opened the letter:

You have been denied admission to the Teaching Credential Program.

In the clouds, a light surrounded me. I thought, "Truly, God loves me!"

I didn't feel this way simply out of relief or just because of the agony I had gone through as a Substitute Teacher. This was something I couldn't explain.

Alice is falling for so long down the rabbit hole that she begins to laugh. Clocks have lost meaning.

I am falling from my sky ship, but start free-falling in my orange jumpsuit.

"Why do skydivers wear helmets?" a comedian is asking me. I throw off my helmet. With goggles on, I smile. The ground is a trampoline. I bounce back into the sky, all the way back up to my ship. I step inside, safe again.

Rejection letters from book publishers kept me humble. I got hundreds. Most wrote, *Not for us.* Or the ever-popular, *It didn't meet our needs at this time but we wish you luck with future writing endeavors.* One rejection letter shook my confidence. "I felt like I was reading *Alice in Wonderland,*" the publisher wrote.

I started to smile. He had compared my story to one of my favorite books. Then:

"Spacing all wrong. Not funny. Not for us."

I re-read some of the cover letters I'd sent out over the years. Most were so full of my boasts, I wondered if anyone had even bothered looking at the stories they went with.

One cover letter described the story as *an all-five inclusive epic comedy: the truest form.* By *all five* I had meant all five senses. Guess I should have explained that in the letter.

If anyone deserved to be tetherball-slapped back to reality, it was me back then, so those rejection letters helped me in many ways. When I did get some acceptance letters, I could appreciate them as connections with editors and the readers of their publications. This felt different from back when my only intention was to prove my greatness as a writer.

In those years, my routine included going to mailbox full of hope, finding a manila envelope with the poems or stories I had submitted, plus a rejection letter. Once, a personal letter stated appreciation for my interest in the magazine, but noted that the publishing company had gone out of business the year before. They had even returned my stories!

Lots of times, all I would get back would be a rejection letter. It was as if the stories I had submitted didn't exist anymore. Still, I kept mailing them out, going to the mailbox every day, sometimes right when the mailman arrived.

My fantasies about being published became silly. I thought that angle – about an acceptance letter revealing the cynical world of publishing – might make a good prose poem:

> Recently I received news that my poem was selected to be showcased at a poetry convention. I was absolutely thrilled. It was only $600 to attend, and Ed Asner and Leslie Nielsen would be there.
>
> It said that there would be a parade in my honor and then I would be awarded the coveted *Trophy of Excellence*. It said Dr. Kenneth Fan, the Poet Laureate of China, would be there.
>
> Then I saw on the internet all these people saying how they went to it and no one was there. So I asked my brother, "Would the best poet out of a billion people be at a poetry convention that doesn't exist?"
>
> And he said "Not even the Poet Laureate of Chinatown."
>
> I never went, but somehow, somewhere, there was a parade in my honor that I was unable to attend.

Pride caused me to put my whole life in the hole. I had always connected with a line from *One Flew Over The Cuckoo's Nest*: "That nurse, she ain't honest. She likes a rigged game. You know what I mean?"

I tried to rig the game of life. I thought I could take the risk out of every situation I came across. I convinced myself that if I kept thinking I was the best (even when reality kept stomping this out of my skull), I could live risk-free. In a poem titled *Adolescence*, I was starting to see this wasn't possible. But the opening line revealed that I believed I could just wish this mindset away: "Adolescence, you are no longer under arrest. You are free to go."

If only it could have been that easy. In one of my first classes as a Substitute Teacher, I turned my back to the room to write something on the blackboard. When I turned around, 90 percent of the students had left. The others were still filing out the door.

Then two students in my class started fighting in the hall. Security Guards broke it up. Watching all of this, I got my first inkling that I was going to have my pride gently beaten out of me.

A dream: students had books that made me remember a comedy show where a hip, young computer company CEO saw a book and said, "Paper? Super throwback!" The kids in my class were holding their books like favorite stuffed animals and were smiling at one another. They made polite conversation that sounded like dishes and cups softly rattling. Then I spoke. They stared at me. I asked them questions. No one answered. I wrote something on the board. No one looked at it. The bell rang. The students didn't move. I picked up my things and went outside for recess.

You're a child in a room full of teachers. You try to find the answers, but can't. So you escape to the playground. If that's what the dream meant, should I quit being a teacher or should I have quit going to school as a student?

I know I wanted to rig the game—to make myself into someone impossible to reject. I needed to get in shape. I needed a tan. And perfect hair. I read books. I tried to get up to date on all current events, all local cultural happenings, all the latest funny movies and shows. If I did this, and if I wore the right clothes, women would come on to me. This started sounding desperate, even to me.

I hadn't been on a date for 13 years. I had asked out a few women, but was rejected each time. I didn't realize then that I couldn't take the risk out of life. So I had to keep asking girls out, because they wouldn't ask me out.

On TV and in movies, the woman would almost always make the first move. If I hadn't been so full of pride, I would have seen these TV shows and movies weren't reflections of real life.

But I kept hearing stories about the Alpha Male walking into places and all the women giving him their phone numbers. I must be a Beta.

I felt like the original VCR player Beta Max: a disappointment. The character Snake on *The Simpsons* steals a home movie theater, then realizes, "Oh no, Beta."

Note to self: Story about a man who thought he was an Alpha but turned out to be a Beta. Do not name him Max.

LIKE VHS AND BETA
HE WAS THE MAN WHO THOUGHT
HE WAS AN ALPHA BUT
TURNED OUT TO BE "BETA"

"Fascinating, the Puff Bird puffs
Up his chest and all the female
birds fly away."

When I took our family golden retriever to obedience school, it pulled me all over the building. The dog would jump on people, knock things over, dragging me the whole time. But when it got in class with a trainer, a woman who described herself as an Alpha, our dog became the star pupil.

Whenever the trainer wanted to show the class the ideal way that a dog should perform an obedience task, she'd snap her fingers and say in a regal voice, "Madison! Come here Madison." And our dog would go right to her and perform the task perfectly.

After class, I would take back the leash and Madison would drag me out of the building, behaving like her old self before I could wrangle her into the car and drive home.

Beta-man lives.

My high school girlfriend re-styled my hair. I had been wearing long bangs, uncombed, because I felt that set me apart. She got me some nice clothes and we worked out a ridiculous amount of time each day. I even went to a tanning booth a few times. I thought, *Now the cool guys will accept me.* I clung to this illusion each time I looked in the mirror. Even 20 years later, I can't wear a shirt that has a pattern similar to a shirt my girlfriend bought me back then, when I'd jokingly tell my reflection, "You're just too much," then blush and feign embarrassment by saying, "Stop it."

That masquerade resembled a *Special K* commercial: a woman tries on jeans and smiles as the narrator says "Slip into size sassy." My girlfriend had gotten rid of the old me and forced me to slip into size sassy. It was the perfect murder. The new Andy didn't look anything like me.

On a dating website page, I used a line from *The Simpsons* when a 2nd grader on a play date with Lisa asks her, "So, do you like stuff?" I got zero responses. I called the dating company to make sure the site was working. A test email replied: *Your site is ready for all kinds of exciting adventures. Let your adventures begin!*

OK, but when?

To perfect my on-paper appeal, I would perfect my voice as an author on these dating sites. Through my writing, I would become flawless in my face-to-face encounters. That's how it would work if I were a Replicant or an Android from *The Terminator*. A newspaper article announced, *Sky Net has not become self aware,* as had been predicted in *The Terminator*.

Perfecting yourself in a vacuum, then taking that to the real world, with real relationships, doesn't work. Life isn't MTV's *The Real World*, where everything is scripted. I still love *Spin City*, the comedy show with Michael J. Fox, whose character says, "I don't think I've seen the Mayor this upset since Puck left *The Real World*."

When I was in this on-paper mentality, I could say the most evil things and think I was just making conversation. When people looked at me funny (this happened a lot), I blamed it on the rules of politeness. I labeled politeness, *conversation's maid.* If I ignored those rules and talked about everything loathsome and terrifying – you know, just friendly conversation with an evil twist – I would demonstrate how interesting I was.

That wasn't the reaction I received.

(I'm still trying to figure out how to get an onion dip and wine stain out of a shirt.)

God blesses us with one thing at a time. We can't handle any more than that. Still, I wonder if we really connect with everything at once.

I don't connect with most of the songs I listen to on the radio, yet there is always one that gets to me at any given time. Does that make every other song crap? No. Just because I don't connect with it now, or ever, doesn't mean others won't connect with it. That song is not the only vessel God is using at the time any of us connect with it. It is God Himself we are connecting with.

This is also true in romance. I had my eyes wide open, looking for many lovers, when God wanted to work through one. This may have caused me to reject *The One* over and over again, standing there with my mouth open, gathering nothing but flies. I'm now ready to cough up those flies and focus on God.

My eyes lied to me and were lied to by others. I no longer worry about that. After all, "The blind receive sight." (*Matthew* 11:5)

Feeling sorry for myself became addicting. The illusion persisted that I could control how I felt: *I can't control how others feel about me, but I can control how I feel.*

How many times had I thought about telling a woman how I felt about her? I always chose the temptation to say nothing. That allowed me to go home and feel sorry for myself. And that made me feel as if I had been in control. But I always felt worse than if I had expressed my feelings and been rejected.

Part of me knew that. My silence served as my security blanket. But I was as insecure and unstable as horses breaking out of a barn in a lightning storm. It would take a long time for me to see that. Presidential candidate Ross Perot helped me down that road.

87

Perot had a lot of sayings to avoid facing an issue: "I'm just saying, you get a pen of chickens and a pig gets in there in the summer, you've got problems."

"But, Mr. Perot," the interviewer would insist, "the question was about taxes."

I needed to answer the questions I was asking myself.

The cyclone sweeps me into a rabbit hole. Wind is charged with lights and the sounds of ships and birds, and I inhale the smell of football practice and rosemary: the charging and the collision of time and space.

The Devil wants to give me a fake wife, and I will have to spend my life with an "I guess so." She will wait beneath a willow tree, among the wind chimes. As I approach her, there will be lightning.

In muffled thunder, I will I fly out to sea.

Like several people I've met, I wondered which character in *The Wizard of Oz* most represented me. It's like a board game some people play. At first, I thought I should pick The Scarecrow, singing *If I Only Had a Brain* and pointing in both directions. Then I switched to The Lion, who also had no courage. I hoped I wasn't The Tin Man, with no heart. I could be the hero, Dorothy. But in the end, I recognized myself in only one character.

Toto.

That little dog isn't responsible for finding its way home. Toto is saved and just along for the ride. Dorothy runs away in the first place because of the Cairn Terrier and finds safety under the bed during the cyclone because of the dog. And Toto pulls the curtain back, revealing the man at the controls of The Wizard.

So – Toto: landing in that beautiful array of flowers, waiting – needing – to be saved.

Definitely me.

When a friend got married a few years back, I wrote her a poem:

> The smashing of two rams,
> a fire in an orchard, the suckling of a lamb:
> love is lava bubbling beneath a crater,
> it carries the power
> and the gentleness of nature.

Every bridesmaid who read it thought it was beautiful, mostly because of its final line, *the gentleness of nature.* I thought groomsmen would like it for its references to the power from *the smashing of two rams.* Wasn't that how it worked – men had power?

Love has all the power.

I had been struck by the old saying, *Love does not become love until it is given away.* Following that adage, I had given myself away most of my life. But giving myself away really meant that I worshipped my would-be lover as an idol, saying whatever she wanted to hear so she would like me, maybe love me. I wasn't giving myself away, I was cowering.

Letting my essence become love was something only God could do. I needed to trust God. It was something He was working on inside me.

The bride and groom I wrote that poem for owned a Golden Retriever, too. Our dogs loved each other and us with a spirit resembling reckless abandon – without fear. Once, I spotted my friend's dog at the edge of high cliff over the ocean. Looking down, the dog leapt into the sea. It was crazy fearless, like *Cliff Diving from Acapulco*, but the dog came out of it safely, like those skilled divers.

Love is more important than fear. Our dogs knew this. I was just beginning to see it.

The problem with art, I thought, was that songs between a man and a woman, were written for a man by a woman, or the other way around:

> *I was in my pajamas and you didn't leave a message,*
> *and I was mad and my friends said I should move on,*
> *but I am still mad and I will just wait and see.*
> *I'm getting up off the couch now to check the fridge.*

Real feelings don't always translate into a good song. Oscar Wilde said that better: "All bad poetry springs from genuine feeling."

I made this mistake constantly when I first started writing and making art. I tossed a pile of my poems into a dumpster while in college. It was all worthless. I had no regrets about trashing it then. Or now.

I've come to see that only God can make art. But back then, songs lived in the halls of my mind, followed me through grocery store aisles: *Leave a message and I will call you back – promise.*

While waiting for those call backs, I learned something. Patience is important, especially with art. Pick the vine too early, get unripe fruit. The wine from that fruit won't be worth drinking. With patience, God will yield good fruit – inside each of us, without our help. We become vessels that God can love through. This is the best life there can be.

That insight made all the waiting worth it – even those times as a Substitute Teacher, when a Principal would fire me, shooting me out of the school like cannon ball, and this after a long day of being humiliated in class by students. I came to expect those moments, waiting for them.

On the clock as a Job Coach, customers in grocery stores would wave their hands in front of my face and say, "Hello! Wake up!" I was a zoner there, too, in another dimension – a land where *My Little Pony* piñatas and *Pikachu* piñatas got along with each other and those tabloids had something to teach me, where candy bars coexisted without any of them being anyone's favorite.

It felt like the dimension of love. It was really only the Waiting Room.

A rt connects humanity and nature. Watching a movie preview with a cartoon wise-cracking parrot, I thought the film would be terrible. Then I saw it, amazed by the way all the nature on screen moved, all those birds and waterfalls. It was like watching the whole of everything.

That preview promoted a disconnect, focusing on hyping those snappy characters. Even with beautiful photography depicting glimpses of the whole, the movie trailer was disconnected from the actual film it was taken from.

I had made this same mistake. In an early essay, I had written:

> *The trees of California remind me of the trees of Connecticut. The trees of Connecticut remind me of Eternity.*

Nature on the East Coast was real. Nature of the West Coast was fake.

From the top of a hill that overlooked the Connecticut town I grew up in, I noticed it had been cut out of the forest around it. From the hill, the few scattered parks in town looked like planted trees.

In Leucadia, a coastal town north of San Diego, a park sits literally in the center divide of a street. It comprises 200 square feet, maybe less. It's what's left of what was.

God brought me back to nature in this tiny park that is smaller than my boyhood back yard in Connecticut. The trees of the Leucadia park breathed, wept, sang, leaves and branches dancing. I spent timeless moments in this park, and hold precious the times I would bring my young nieces to play on the tire swing there. We felt like adventurers, and I began to see that trees didn't make the impact, it was God's spirit that imbued life.

My realm became that tiny roadside park planted in the middle of suburbia. I shared it with our Golden Retrievers. Squirrels would come out to chirp at us, taunting the dogs. When one would give chase, the squirrel would burrow immediately, untouched. A friend once called out a high-pitched squirrel call, making all the squirrels turn and stand on hind legs to stare at us.

We had become the entertainment.

We got pretty good at that. Chasing our Golden Retriever, Madison, and yelling, "Come back here, put it down," I ran into a group of women joggers . One of them reached down to pet the dog. I shouted, "Don't! He has a dead rat in his mouth!" The jogger recoiled and led her friends away at a gallop.

Instinctively, Madison chased them. It's amazing how fast a person can run when rats become part of the equation.

On a biking trip to Canyon Lands Park, Utah, we needed a four wheel-drive vehicle to reach the remote park. A young woman in our group told us she had gotten lost around here once. Without food or water for five days, she had survived on water from puddles. As dangerous as this area might be, it was also stunningly beautiful.

The friends who had invited me forgot to mention that once we reached the park, we would begin a 120-mile bike trip. No way was I in shape to do this. They would stop at scenic points to admire the view: "I wonder what this view is called?" one of them would say.

Breathless, I'd mutter, "It's called Who the Hell Point, as in Who the Hell signed me up for this trip!"

For the last leg of the biking trek, we were supposed to ride switchbacks up a mountain. Fortunately, even my friends agreed that was too much, so we drove up.

Mountain to the left, cliff to the right. Nothing resembling a guard rail anywhere. And down the mountain came a lone Big Horn sheep. It stopped near the front bumper, took one look at us, and leapt off the cliff.

In shock, I suddenly realized that this Big Horn wasn't fazed. It had probably landed 20 feet down on a small crevice. I remember wondering, *How could I ever witness this and claim that I understand nature?*

A similar feeling found me while feeding ducks, when some seagulls showed up. The gulls dominated the ducks. It was like watching *Finding Nemo*, where all the animals can speak, but the seagulls only say, "Mine, Mine." Seagulls make feeding them a sport: toss bread in the air and they'll grab it on the fly.

Then I noticed a crane standing near the battle of gulls vs. ducks. A piece of bread floated near the big bird, but it didn't fight for it. It just looked at it. Maybe, I thought, cranes didn't eat Whole Wheat 7-Grain. Rye might be more their style. Or Oatmeal.

The nobility of that stoic bird convinced me that cranes are the sentinels of the natural world. Emulating them would be a way to experience patience, to wait to see what was really out there.

Baby owls also fascinated me. Adult owls appear as ancient, wise creatures. Their babies are the opposite, and often hilarious. As a young man, I felt like one of these immature owls. I knew nothing, but I thought I had innate wisdom – so much of it that I became a fool. A book of my philosophy in those years would have been titled, *No duh.*

In a story then called *The Obvious*, I recalled being confounded by the deluded awesomeness of my own thoughts. It reminded me of a collection of terrible writing from that same year: *The Worst Articles of the Year*. One paragraph sampled an essay that used the word *therefore* 12 times. This made me laugh – more of a maddening laugh, as if I was letting go of this stage of craziness in my life. The more I re-read this paragraph, the more I laughed. I felt like a baby barn owls in a tree, screaming with the parakeets.

When a bird lands in a garden fountain, it can only genuflect and be filled with gratitude for the fresh water. The garden links to something ancient, with sculptures and stone faces that lead to small caves, near trellises that provide shade. The birds eat, drink, bathe, fly off. The cycle repeats.

Nature is a mystery. In our arrogance, we observe mating rituals and think we understand them. A black bird makes its blue belly puff up to three times the size of its skeleton, then flaps its wings to impress the female. Why does the female choose this male and not another? Some scientists claim the strongest stock gets chosen, but don't smaller rams win battles sometimes?

God chooses the right male, the right ram, because He gives us our fight. I carried a false understanding out into the dating world. I puffed up my chest, thinking, *If I impress girls, they will choose me to fall in love with.* But love, like nature, is a mystery. Do we *decide* who we fall in love with, or does it simply happen?

This scared me the most about the dating world. I tried to control it, just like everything else in my life. And, just like everything else in my life, I failed. I worked out, trying to be the strongest guy, sure that this would impress girls. But all strength is God's: *He is not impressed by the strength of a horse; He does not value the power of a man.* (Psalm 47:10)

I was trying to be an idea of me instead of simply being me.

That was the moral of every teen movie I had ever seen: *Be yourself.* It took 40 years for me to learn that lesson.

I'm still learning. While no longer the blue-bellied black bird puffing up only to watch all the females fly away, I have never fallen in love. I love women and have been inspired more by women than by men. Platonic love seems simpler to me than romantic love, where I built a wall of bitterness that grew taller with each disappointment.

Now I have finally started to see women without a muddied reflection, without that self-created bitterness. I can truly love a woman, and I truly want to.

e better to be the same. No amount of success could ever make me loveable. It might even make me less loveable. The minute I got success, I might have adopted the attitude that what others thought no longer mattered. My success would make other opinions obsolete.

While waiting for that success, I convinced myself I was the exception. I practiced looks in the mirror, like Zoolander. My facial expressions could make people feel things. Deep down, I knew that God's spirit moved through everything. He had blessed me with the ability to make these movie-quality facial expressions, but I took all the credit.

I joined a photographic gallery and paid to have my pictures displayed for sale. One member of the group told me he owned a Canon GX11 still frame camera. I told him, "I have a flip phone."

The ladies who ran that gallery hated my photographs. It made me feel that they also hated me. I printed my flip phone photos through my home computer. Local frame shops didn't carry 8 ½ x 11 frames, only 8 1/2 x 10. So I used scissors to cut the photos to fit that smaller frame size. My uneven scissor work sometimes left open spaces in the framed photos. I never earned a prize or even an Honorable Mention. Toward the end of the first year I finally found some 8 ½ by 11" frames. One of the ladies who ran the place told me, "At least your framing has improved."

Pride deceived me. The key to this deception would become clear: I was the exception, the one person who could do what only God could do. Then I recognized that everybody at this photographic gallery was deceiving themselves the same way. That led me to accept that I couldn't be the exception – not if everyone else was.

Wandering around grocery stores, scanning covers of magazines, I began thinking, *That cover model is deceiving herself. Her proud look wouldn't make anyone feel anything.* I might as well have been a fish, swimming through the grocery store aisles, following a baited lure.

I developed theories: actors got accepted in Hollywood because they believed the lie of The Devil, deceiving themselves that they had power they really didn't possess. I'd see an actress on a magazine cover and think, *That poor child. Doesn't she know she's being deceived?* Then I'd stroll the aisles thinking, *But not me. I'm way too smart for that. Hey, what kind of chips are these? I wonder if they're any good.*

I waited for someone to recognize me and ask to take my picture. I imagined puffing up: "Here, get my silhouette! My profile! Can you make a copy for me? "

And I would offer to autograph the photo, which, I would insist, should be titled, *Andy Palasciano: The Exception.*

Fortunately, even while I was experiencing this delusion, I was also starting to accept how special I was not: *Andy: No Exception.* In true blockhead style, I invented what I thought was a new word to commemorate this moment:

The Acception

Saying someone is
a great artist
is like calling
a bullfrog
Bill Fernandez

Exceptional-Non-Exceptional Andy had not realized that the word *acception* actually existed, and that it meant exactly the same thing as my pseudo-invention — *a particular sense, or the generally recognized meaning of a word or phrase.*

So ended my short-lived career as Coiner-of-Words.

T he whole time at that photographic gallery, I sold one $10 box of greeting cards, made from my photos. After I had applied for and received a seller's permit at City Hall, I was told $10 was too small of an amount to declare. And I cancelled my seller's permit immediately and haven't had one since.

That measly $10 sale didn't stop me from dreaming big. In a poem, *The American Dream Gone Haywire*, I created a list: Genius, Great Artist — all the things I was certain I would be recognized as. The final line of that poem: *And they will have to like me.*

As pathetic as this was, I couldn't stop striving for things to add to that list. Great Surfer was the next one. The first day at my proving grounds in Carlsbad, graffiti on a wall at the beach warned me: *Dude, Bail!*

I started on a short board, too proud to have to learn on a long board. I would shred the first wave I caught, become an instant legend. Small problem: I'm a big guy and on that short board, I just sank, unable to catch a wave because my board was under water.

For about a year, I tried but I didn't catch a single wave. I would paddle out and tell other surfers, "Yeah, I shred mittens." Failing to shred anything but my ego, I'd go to my parents' house, take the elevator to the roof, sit in a hot tub overlooking the ocean, still wearing my surfer clothes. A fraud, and terrified of being revealed as *The One Who Does Not Shred Mittens*, I'd drive my nice car in my rad surfer clothes, never making a real friend. I was too afraid of being unmasked as a fake. All the while, I dreamt of bragging that this was my beach house, and how I could shred mittens. I never got a single date.

Then the best thing happened: I moved out of the area and never tried to surf again, or wear surfer clothes. I had finally heeded the writing on the wall: *Dude, I Bailed!*

C omedy is a great thing. Laughter is a response to new energy. God gives us this new energy so we can live and love. But I used comedy to avoid all risk.

I practiced my comedy routines at parties, believing that if I demonstrated I was funnier than everyone else, the risk of rejection would be gone. At the very least, their opinions would no longer matter to me. It never occurred to me that what they thought of me might never have mattered to begin with.

Where others used comedy to open doors, I used it as a way to shut them. Yet another attempt in a long series of upside-down thinking, to get people to like me.

I saw a sign
    that said
    Donuts
    They're better than you think

And I screamed so loud
    that I couldn't
    look a baby in the eye

We'll take credit for
the light and suffer
its shadows
      Signed,
      Satan's Caveman

Mom! Plato threw
me in a cave

Plato!

A s a would-be guitar teacher, I named my approach, *The Living Guitar*, subtitled, *It's time to stop playing and time to start living with your guitar.*

It would have helped if I had known more than two chords and didn't have to stop between each chord change to get my fingers in position. I had taken lessons. My teacher laughed and told me, "You've got to just let it happen naturally."

The guitar, like everything else, did not come naturally to me.

I still remember those two chords and I play melodies with one or two strings. I shouldn't have been giving lessons on guitar or anything else. When God wants to move, He moves. I had to learn to be open to Him.

I had amassed a string of unsuccessful endeavors:

    Great stand-up comic – failed
    Great surfer – failed
    Great photographer – failed
    Great artist – failed
    Great guitarist/teacher – failed

With each new venture, my motive remained constant: excel and everyone, especially girls, will like me. I was a slow learner.

I went to six different colleges before graduating with a Bachelor's Degree. At four state colleges, I averaged one semester. Each time, I expected results just like in the movies: I'd blossom and live in glory. That didn't play out.

When I left each college, I blamed others. "The people there weren't real," I would tell anyone who would listen. My heart was angry.

My brother and his friend appear as extras in the 1987 movie *Teen Wolf Too*. I wasn't even an extra in my own life. I couldn't catch a Frisbee in my teeth, I couldn't be hip. My college movie wasn't awesome. It was unwatchable — and in those days, I would watch anything.

I seemed to be wandering through my personal version of *The Twilight Zone*. Slowly, I began to realize that life couldn't be real life without any risk. The adult me had been ignoring the real me — that inner child me. I tackled that in a poem, *The Myth of Manhood*, seeing that the new me wasn't me at all.

When my girlfriend broke up with me, back when we were in our 20's, she told me, "You're a shell."

I thought, *Wow, like I have a candy-coated shell. I'm delicious!*

I was that self-absorbed. Then God pointed out that I was not on the menu. Any menu. Instead, I was a Russian Nesting Doll, smaller versions within each shell. The final doll, the smallest, is the most vulnerable. It needs to trust that something greater will protect it.

With each of my failures, a smaller and smaller Andy came out.

A t Plymouth Plantation in Massachusetts with my cousin and her two young children, we had to push a stroller and carry a two year-old over a mile of dirt paths to reach the village to experience re-enactments of the lives of Pilgrims. These actors were so convincing, the two year-old finally screamed, "Mommy, this is not a good place!"

On our way out, it started raining, with lightning. I asked a costumed actor how to get back to the exit. "It be up yonder," she said. We got soaked and the stroller got muddy trying to find *up yonder*. My cousin sighed in the car: "Those reenactors just don't let it go."

That's how I have come to see my persistent struggles to be the best: I just couldn't let it go.

My painful experiences taught me that the key to any endeavor is to understand that you are probably terrible at it. It can be art or teaching or even finding your car in a rain and lightning storm – anything. The path to becoming a great photographer, one used by God, begins with the realization that no one is born with a camera in his hand. The craft, the art, has to be learned. I've learned that failure is part of the journey, and that nothing can be done successfully without God.

God can do anything. We can do nothing. Talent will always defeat skill, and talent comes out when God uses us. Skill, on the other hand, is a practiced thing, like when I try to somersault off a diving board into a swimming pool, but and wind up doing a belly flop instead, and suffer a red chest all day.

E ach of us has a set-up song in our life. An R.E.M. fan wouldn't hope the band played *Underneath the Bunker* at a concert. Instead, the fan would hope to hear a big hit, like *Flowers of Guatemala*. But set-up songs prepare us for the bigger things, the great things.

So many moments in my life serve as my set-up songs. I've learned to be grateful they exist.

In *Common Sense*, Thomas Paine discusses how we laugh at things that we have outgrown. The original colonies were laughing at British rule because they had outgrown it. Being governed from across the ocean had become a yoke. The growing demand for freedom among the Colonists had made British rule untenable. Their ridicule of King George III – The Mad King – indicated that he was irrelevant to the concept of independence.

I had come to a stage in my life when years of failures now felt painfully funny. I could laugh at them, and myself, because I had finally stopped using the wrong motives to take on new endeavors. Once upon an Andy, I might have bought a pair of goldfish to see if I could breed an army of super goldfish that might help me rule the world – or at least impress a girl. I learned to let go.

The foam seahorse nestled
in my hand in the bathtub.
I remembered in school
how the Entrepreneur that I was
was assigned to do a report on
King Camp Gillette,
who campaigned hard through books,
charts and speeches to have
everyone move to underwater Bubble Villages
where he would be king.
Then he had a vision of disposable razors,
sold them,
then went back to campaigning
to be king of underwater cities.
I looked at my seahorse
and imagined riding it to my underwater kingdom
and thought if he could, then
maybe I could, too.
Then I watched the bubbles
go down the drain
and was suddenly glad my mom
gave us tearless shampoo.

Not every lesson learned was that terrible. Each new endeavor brought some joy because I felt closer to God. There were moments of intense fear and humiliation, but I was being gently let down, like when I got on the roof as a boy. My mom let me back inside through a window. Any punishment I received was still better than falling off the roof.

My Journey of The Heart, back to being
who I've always been, wasn't like going into
The Heart of Darkness. With Christ carrying
me, it's more like being on the Disneyland ride,
Twenty Thousand Leagues Under the Sea,
and looking out of the bubbled glass
and saying "Ooh, sea monsters. "

What hurts most is the deflation. I would puff myself up, deluding myself that every time someone met me they thought I was the funniest, best looking guy they had ever met. I would hear people saying things as I left a party, and persuaded myself that I heard them saying, "Who was that? He was amazing!" Then a pin would pop my balloon. That hurt my pride because it revealed I had been wrong. Through those years, my pride got hurt a lot.

In high school a girl told me that her classmate didn't think I was good looking. She said this girl thought my head was too small for my body. It felt like something out of the movie *Tommy Boy*, where Chris Farley got told he was a big guy with a tiny head, and, in disbelief, responded, "I have a tiny head?"

Still, I would cling to compliments as though holding on to a ledge. People would tell me, "You're amazing. Everyone likes you, don't believe any criticism." I don't know what was worse, the world lying to me or that I believed those lies.

P ositivity is not realistic. I believe in it, but being realistic makes me joyful of all the good things. I no longer see all the bad things as downers, things that never should have happened. Trying to be positive all the time eventually dragged me down.

I was only joyful about the positive things. No one likes the bad things that happen, but when I began to see how a higher power in my life was guiding me to overcome these negative experiences, I began to learn from them. That helped me see them as valuable, and proof that God was teaching me.

The difference between being positive and being delusional also became clear. The delusional me saw the positive, but also saw a world unrelated to reality. I believed I was being accepted to such a degree that it went against the Higher Power in my life, the force that could defeat my delusion. I had become my worst enemy, needing a false sense of superiority. Part of me had to know how deluded this was, because every time I acted like a puffer fish in a tiny bowl, somebody stuck a pin in me, popping all the air out.

Before getting popped, I was always waiting to be discovered – by a modeling agency, a magazine, a talent scout, a beautiful woman. I was a goldfish placed in a small bowl by someone who was telling me, "Ok, now, pretend it's the ocean!"

101

One thing I learned: I'm a terrible actor. People kept telling me to act my age. I was never up to that role.

Thankfully, God knew my heart, so I no longer have to act any more. Of course, I never actually had to act. I had deluded myself into thinking I had to become some ideal person in order to impress others. My mannered life had turned me into the "skim-coat or finish of falsehood" that Thoreau wrote about in his journal of 1858, when he was about my age. I had become one of those "not brave enough to do without this sort of armor, which they wear night and day."

I am so happy I shed that restrictive armor, that finish of falsehood.

I had been trying to do what only God could do. He let me fail again and again. God brought me down to the ground so I could walk. The Icarus wings I had made out of Play Doh were melting.

There were no complications at my birth. I was born into this world healthy. But I complicated life.

Love is not complicated, yet I tried for years to oversimplify its already simple and elegant nature. When I tried to take the risk out of love, I removed trust. Life without risk becomes a video game, but, as overheard on MTV, "In real life you don't get another quarter."

In a documentary, Igor Sikorsky, who pioneered the helicopter, was described as a brilliant engineer, writer, scientist, and physicist. I wanted to be thought of like that, someone who could do it all. I would learn, however, with each new failure, that I couldn't do anything without God.

The remake of the movie *Journey to the Center of the Earth* features the main character describing his missing brother as one of those rare people who was amazing at everything he did. Being impressionable, I thought maybe I was amazing, too. As I failed over and over, I began to feel as though someone was forcing me through a Play-Doh spaghetti masher for cooking in an Easy Bake Oven. It would eventually occur to me that this someone was me.

Looking through a haze of confetti at the kids in a kindergarten class I was teaching, I finally got it:

"Maybe it's just The Mets and Spider Man who are amazing."

To me, someone who gets labeled "a legend" is someone used by God. People wonder where this legend's talent or genius came from. To most, that remains a mystery. Not to me. I know it comes from God.

A critic writing about T.S. Eliot proclaimed the greatness of the English poet as being many times that of any other poet. This struck me has hilarious. That kind of greatness belongs only to God. We are His vessels—even a "legend" like T.S. Eliot. Or Zorro.

5

My Gerbil
Birthrite

For a while, I thought overpopulation was the problem. In a story, I described a city set up with giant nets between buildings – hammocks that the millions of people slept in because there was no housing, no room for them. Massive monsters attacked this city, threatening the citizens the same way I thought monsters were tormenting my life. I came to see that these giants represented the tiniest of fears.

The menacing monsters, with eyes the size of manhole covers, stood hundreds of feet tall. They were really the size of Smurfs. That realization caused me, Blockhead Smurf, to drop his wooden mallet and feel foolish. These monsters were kids.

Deep down, I was still a kid.

Not a hero fighting giants, not a champion raising Excalibur in glory, I was shown by God that these monsters were small gerbils, pets I didn't need to entertain. Instead, I could chuckle at how cute they were and let them out of their cages. The Great Gerbil Rebellion had been routed.

And just in time.

For years I had felt like a gerbil in a glass cage, with everyone watching me, not allowing me to be free and live my life. I had to be shown that I had been my own jailer. Now, the wheel inside that glass cage stood empty.

M any people claim to be dream warriors. Victorious in dreams, they feel victorious in life. Some claim to fly in their dreams. Others score goals and become the leading scorer on their water polo team. My dreams used to be characterized by molasses.

I was always stuck in that dark goo: powerless, an absolute mole to everyone else, controlled by all of them. Fly? In my dreams, I couldn't even walk.

"Since this is my dream," I would keep saying, "can I ask a question?"

"No!"

"OK, sorry. I was just wondering. Hey, that's the first classroom I ever taught in! Can I go in there?"

"No!"

"OK, I'll just swing on the swing set out here."

"No swinging!"

"OK, I'll just sit on the swing then and wait for you."

"I will be a very long time!"

"That's OK, I can wait."

By itself, molasses tastes bittersweet. So did my dreams.

I n one dream as a kid, a steamroller flattened me. Then my brother told on me, saying I had crossed the street by myself. Not only flattened, I was now going to get punished.

Dreams like that spilled into my reality. In my dreams, my powerlessness was legendary.

Feral cats screamed like babies, tormenting my sleep, growing into giants from their voices. By contrast, my brother dreamt he saw a leprechaun, running past the bathroom door and down the hall. Why did I make something small, like a cat, into something so big and ominous?

So that I could defeat them and become a hero.

In epic tales, the hero faced monsters, becoming stronger through those battles and winning in the end. I fought, but my monsters just wouldn't die.

One of my most vivid dreams came as an adult. At a school assembly, I was the Substitute Teacher of the Day. I sat on stage, over a dunk tank. The Principal told the kids in the audience, "Now is the time of mockery! Mock this man!"

The children gave no reaction. In the silence, the Principal pulled a lever. I plummeted in to water, which crackled with sparks of light. Electric eels of many colors – purple, blue, brown – swam by me. I dove to escape, got caught in a whirlpool.

Down below, a giant creature floated past. *Nautilus*, Captain Nemo's submarine? Divers in prehistoric space suits walked on the ocean floor. One of them said, "Release the Kraken!"

I hid in tall trees of kelp. But I was glowing turquoise – easy to spot. Sure enough, a long-haired man holding a trident nodded at me. "How long can I stay down here?" I asked, realizing that I could breathe somehow (encouraging). And there were jellyfish to eat (sweet tooth). I waved to the man with the trident and swam deeper, into darkness.

A lantern fish swam by and sat atop a lamp pole. I swam into the light. An entire street was lit by lantern fish on poles. I walked up the cobblestones, passed sea cows on the side of the road. Coaches pulled by horses rolled past. Children peered out the coach windows, their smiles turning to indifference. It felt like an underwater England.

I kept swimming toward the strange light on the horizon.

"Don't worry," my brother told me, "everyone goes through a period of fear."

I didn't want compassion. I wanted to be seen as unique. If everyone was going through the same thing, how could I be an original? I had to hold on to these giant fears so that I could defeat them.

Jellyfish, it turned out, were not the only brainless creatures in the sea.

Imagine a battle where compliments are more dangerous than insults. Armies sit in trenches. Barrages of compliments and insults are exchanged across the battlefield:

"You're a silly goose!"

"You're a nincompoop!"

Soldiers duck and regroup. A cannon gets loaded. It fires. The cannonball explodes like a firework above the enemy trench and announces, "Your nails are cute!"

Enemy soldiers fall to their knees, hold their hearts. They are defeated and they know it. A flag of victory is planted by the other side.

This, I would come to understand, was a way to make peace with my bitterness toward women. As a teenager, I couldn't get a date. I wound up questioning why I should feel compassion for women, when they had never shown me an ounce of compassion by making it easier for me to get a date. At the root of my giant fears around women was a teenage boy, alone and feeling foolish.

I needed to send good thoughts across this battlefield. Back then, I didn't know how.

And I didn't know how for a long time.

A high school psychology class required us to close our eyes and visualize a dream scenario. Dreams full of light were supposed to be more mature than dreams of darkness. My girlfriend, seated next to me, saw herself walking through a forest full of bright beauty. I saw myself tumbling down a dark staircase.

"Really?" she said. "I dreamed of a lighted forest."

"Thanks for waking me up when you did," I told her. "I might have kept tumbling and hurt myself."

Part of me was glad she wasn't with me in my dream. Part of me was sad for her that I wasn't with her in hers.

107

My family helped me buy a car at an auction. The Pontiac Firebird cost $2000. It had a shade guard on the back window with *The Shadow* printed on it. As a high school kid, I didn't know too much about cars, so when someone asked what kind of car I drove, I said, "A Shadow."

The cool kids took this as a joke, but at my expense. They started calling my car *The Shadow* from then on.

That car had some issues. The first week, it stopped running. The mechanic said it needed a new master cylinder. That would cost $1500. The next week, the transmission went out. A month or so later, I fell asleep at the wheel, crashing into a fence pole, then bouncing off into a tree. This solved the mechanical issues.

Looking at The Shadow in the junkyard, it didn't seem possible that anyone could have survived that crash. The pole had punctured the back seat. The tree had crushed the front passenger seat. Moments prior to that crash, I had dropped my girlfriend off at her house. God had been with us, I thought, touching the mangled steel.

Seeing the wreck, touching it, reminded me of the night before the crash. I had stepped out of the car feeling as if I had been in a space ship. One headlight seemed to be facing in one direction, the other in a different direction. I thought I had felt blood on my skull.

Suddenly, I was wondering if I had died that night. Was the life I was living now the creation of my mind? An alternate reality?

My mom's hug brought me back to the junkyard. "I'm glad you made it."

Just as quickly, I started doubting that hug. Was this person really my mother, or was I imagining her, this junkyard, that car?

The fear I felt in that moment had an effect on me for a long time. Even to this day, 26 years later, I wonder if I will wake up and see headlights facing different directions.

This helped me understand why combat veterans with PTSD need hugs to bring them out of their nightmares. We're all scared kids, aren't we?

A dream about looking back at times in my life: my genuine successes didn't come when I was most productive. The times I didn't try to hold onto each grain of sand slipping out of the hour glass were the moments of greatest joy.

Learning how to surrender to the moment would take more time, more dreams. But I would learn:

I raise my fist to the clatter. I'm sure if it mattered, it wouldn't matter.

I used to think Mothra was Godzilla's friend. The turtle powered by fire was actually named Gamera. I must have been confused about a lot things related to Godzilla, because every time I would watch the movie and hear its cry in the distance, I found myself in a store with Grandfather clocks. One of the clocks had the name of a soccer teammate on it: *Seth*. All the clocks chimed 4 o'clock. Cuckoos popped out of some of them. I would wake up back in the middle of the Godzilla movie.

Only years later did I learn that Seth Thomas had been a master clock maker. He died before the Civil War started, but his company continued into the 21st Century. The *Seth Thomas* name appeared as a signature logo on the face of all clocks the company made.

Monsters like Godzilla, like my fears, were stealing the most valuable thing I owned: time.

The lady at the school's Lost and Found told me, "We don't sell donuts."

I walked away, a hungry Substitute Teacher. A young girl in my class shoots me a quizzical look. Reflected in her eyes I see the futility of my daily toil.

That dream snippet jarred me into questioning what kept me getting up to go to work all that time, with no chance of success, no plan or hope of success? I decided it had to be the allure of failure.

Failure is addicting because it's so easy to attain. Do nothing and fail. How special could I be if anyone could match my failures?

I sometimes consider people as fellow babies in the newborn ward. As I look around, I realize that all of this—the telephone poles, trees, the sidewalks—is simply life outside the womb, as if a loudspeaker had reverberated, "Come on out."

When a storm downs power lines, I imagine a baby staring out the window, past a man holding a microphone and wearing a t-shirt with *The World* printed across the front. The baby's crib has a rhyme painted on it:

> A Catcher, Catcher in the Rye,
> The World has always been out there,
> and it has always been a lie.

We're all looking for a safe place. At some point, we learn that we have to be involved in creating it.

Alice In Wonderland is one of my favorite books. Years ago, if a famous critic had told me it wasn't any good, I might have thought that I could have been fooling myself when I read it. Maybe I hadn't enjoyed it after all.

Believing critics can be dangerous. God is not a critic.

> Nothing lives under the critical eye.
> I tried to grow petunias,
> but they all died.

The circus tent is packed with kids from my classes as a Substitute Teacher. The Ringmaster raises a megaphone:
> "Aim your slander, but don't pander.
> Take a gander at the center of the ring
> and the cannonball we are about to fling."

I am that cannonball.

The match is lit, the fuse burns. With a *boom*, I get shot across the arena, flying toward a giant net. The look on the kids' faces convinces me that they wish me no harm. I try to return that look. Then I land in the net, bounce up toward the big top, then back into the net, back up, back down. I crawl out, plant my feet on the ground. The kids don't listen to the Ringmaster. They cheer.

One dream created an important turning point for me: A fire alarm goes off in the sky, activating the sprinkler system. I am a child riding on the front of a shopping cart. It might be a cart being pushed by someone else's mom, but it no longer matters. I decide that I don't want anyone to live my life only for myself. I spread my arms out. Rain hits my face. Instantly, I become a fan of the rain. Cannot get enough of it.

My college computer lab didn't permit the use of flash drives. The professor called that "like having a room full of toasters, but no food allowed!" We studied fallacies. The part-whole fallacy stated that just because you liked all the ingredients of a recipe for a meal doesn't guarantee you would like the meal itself.

I thought I knew the recipe for art. If I used a sure-fire ingredient, success would be guaranteed. If there is such a recipe, I now know that it is known only to God.

The Straw Man Fallacy gives the sense of arguing a point, but not a point the opponent has raised. I saw the Straw Man on a cross, with fruit growing below him. How many times had I attacked an innocent in my attempt to be cool, to be superior? I have never been violent, but my comments have hurt people. Trying to succeed without God hurt others even when I was unaware of it. God's patience cleansed me along the way. Still, I missed out on a lot. Until that dream rain:

Rain on the scarecrow's lake keeps the sun in its wake.

I had been in a flood, now swept from the place where I had been my own worst enemy, a place where my words had been my undoing, heading toward a place God would bridle my tongue and give me a new song.

I went to the record store to see how my new CD was selling. The rack was full. Thinking everyone must truly love my music, I noticed where the store had place the rack: *The Used Section*. I hated that dream.

A college roommate used to say, "Everyone is in their own universe." Young and impressionable, I believed it. Soon, it developed into a fear. I began thinking, *I sneezed the other day and caused that tornado in Thailand. Sorry about that.*

Worried that my moods caused natural disasters, I related my concern to a psychiatrist who had also been the Chaplain at a hospital where I had been placed in the psychiatric ward. She looked at me and said, "You really are confusing identities with God."

"OK, but help me figure this out so we can stop all these natural disasters."

She didn't show up for my next appointment and never returned my phone calls. I remember hoping that one of my bad moods hadn't killed her.

T he world is imperfect. Imperfection is God's gift to us. If we were perfect in a perfect world, we would be God. That would be a nightmare.

In college, I wrote a poem: *The Wallpaper We Came from Is White.* I thought I could become perfect and stay catatonic inside white wallpaper forever. Madness. (The sign on my dorm room read, *Stop The Madness.*) I favored not being a madman, but I lost the vote.

Maybe I shouldn't have filibustered.

I n High School I held a job briefly at a department store. Nothing on the shelves. All products were upstairs, in the warehouse. A conveyer belt sent the purchased items to the checkout area.

On my floor – the sales floor – customers examined models of every item. Model numbers got entered by customers into a computer. The warehouse would fulfill the order. The computer system, however, was imperfect.

Sometimes, the computer showed an item as *available* when it was *out of stock* upstairs. Around the holidays, customers would punch in their orders, wait for an hour in line to get to the cashier and show the item number they wanted to purchase. I was that cashier.

At the conveyor belt, I would find a little note: *Out of Stock.* Nothing brought the holidays home like a furious customer.

Because I was not what anyone would call the most customer-friendly guy in those days, and because I was so bad with numbers and messed up so many orders, I got demoted to Conveyor Belt Boy. Never had a demotion brought so much joy.

Of course, Conveyor Belt Boy had been a totally made-up position, just for me. I got fired shortly after New Year's. That holiday season, I began to see myself as a grinning in-stock floor model who, in reality, was out-of-stock emotionally.

A few years later, I created a Christmas website, displaying my photos and writing. I also built a short poem out of quotes from a friend who grew up on a farm:

> There were bobcats,
> and there were bicycle chain bits,
> steel in the doubletree
> from here to Summerset.

My friend's animals had broken a wooden doubletree used to hitch a pair of mules. Those mules couldn't break the steel doubletree. They could pull a truck out of a ditch in that rig.

I identified with those mules, straining against that steel doubletree, yet all the while admiring the sunset.

S ometimes, I would end up in the hospital around Christmastime because I would push myself to get presents for everyone I was friends with. It took several holiday seasons for me to recognize the pattern of having a breakdown and seeing the same Christmas angels decorating the same hospital again.

On the hospital elevator door, a picture of young children as angels with a finger to their lips indicated *Quiet*. That always made me hear *Deck The Halls* in my mind and made me want to dance around the Christmas tree in the hospital lobby.

Around this time, I began to associate Christmas with classical music. *The Nutcracker Suite*. Any Tchaikovsky piece played by violinist Jascha Heifetz. Marc Chagall's art. These became favorites, driving forces that led me home. Home is the place for the Holidays, and it is the place God would lead me to stay all year round.

For a while, I dreamed of owning and running a printing press. I envisioned a hard-working, loyal staff, a thriving business printing art. The sign in the front window the shop would read, *Always go at the speed of God.*

I had calculated Godspeed at one mile per hour. The speed of the world came in a 10 miles per hour. Studying with a friend who owned a printing press, I figured out that a staff operating at one mile per hour would get nothing done.

Working in my printing shop would resemble being in an above-ground pool, with leaves that had fallen from trees on the water. Playing with others – my staff – the game of tag could get loud with yelling that bounced off the sliding glass door of the house – the shop – where inside a TV would be on, the volume too low to make out the sounds. Pressed against the wall of the pool, everyone would agree on something, form a line and run in a circle, creating a cyclone of water. I would let go of the side of the pool, get caught in the vortex, start spinning.

I quit the printing business while I was still above water.

Ever since my high school girlfriend picked out my clothes, I have been more an outfit walking down the street than a man. The shrine of clothes in my closet made me who I was. My fake reality collapsed when I got rid of those outfits. Those clothes had worn me.

Sadly, a residue of those days still exists. When I wear clothes similar to the ones my old girlfriend chose, I feel myself puff up and begin to think, "I'm a little beyond this place. I'm sassy."

That reference to a *Saturday Night Live* sketch, with Phil Hartman as editor of *Sassy Magazine*, now serves as a reminder of the fake me I had created and all those outfits had tried to sustain.

One surfer outfit in particular caused me major stress. I knew I was a fraud wearing it. When I found those clothes on the floor one morning, I was tempted to burn them. I threw them out instead.

Every day should be Halloween or Guy Fawkes Day: a motto I believed once, sure that people should be free to wear any costume they wanted. The day after Halloween, why dress normally again? Why wear the costume of an everyday life? Why take that everyday life so seriously?

114

I can't blame my high school girlfriend. She only brought out the pride I already had. I feared my everyday costume, those outfits she had picked out for me, because I felt they had power. I started feeling like The Beatles escaping a mob of adoring girls, but when I looked back around the corner, no mob filled the empty street.

I had been staring at my own reflection in the lake. Someone threw a rock at water just to watch me run. And the rock thrower was me.

This is why philosophers should use the word *I* instead of *We*. And even though it is grammatically incorrect English, they should use the word *me*, as in, *It's me*, not, *It is I*.

I did it. It was me.

Some blame rejection, or tough classes, or cell phones, or boredom. Not me. I did evil because I chose to. It's that simple. I blame my pride.

I've had bad influences in my life, but I never believed others could do things that I didn't believe I could also do. I needed God. I had to stop blaming others for my sins before I could grow. I had to stop saying, "We do this" and start admitting, "I do this."

Schools and universities taught me how to think, but they couldn't teach me to stop thinking. That trick came from God. My mind would run like a steam locomotive and I was powerless to stop it. On walkabout, I'd stroll through my neighborhood, sometimes beyond it. Periodically, a breakdown would send me to the psyche ward at the hospital.

In one of those breakdowns, I had a vision. The voice of Jesus, perfect Son of God, told me, "Because you have desired me, your sins are forgiven." Accounts of visions like this are common to every religion, every culture, every time period. The result is a form of salvation. It certainly felt that way to me.

I still experienced fear after that, but it felt different. I knew that God had it covered and had forgiven all of my sins – past, present and future. God knew it all and still forgave me. For the first time in my life, I was all paid up.

When my brother worked in L.A., he would recount the freeways he had to take each day to avoid as much traffic as possible: "I took the 5 to the 57 to the 10 to the 60 to the 215."

Some days, he would name a dozen freeways, going up and coming driving back. One freeway was so dark, with traffic so terrifying, he and I agreed never to speak its name. (It's the 101)

We'd joke that the 405 got its name because rush-hour traffic moved at 4 or 5 miles per hour. One Saturday morning, we drove a traffic-free 405 and my brother had tears in his eyes. "It's beautiful", he said, pulling out his phone to take a video of something he was sure he would never see again.

I had felt the same way leaving the psyche ward after my vision For once, I wasn't strangling my own life. I was sailing down a river, filled with hope and love.

It was beautiful.

Some old dreams still confuse me. In one, I open a cabinet marked *Honey* in a tree house. Inside, I find no honey, only a note that reads, *An eternal work is a work eternal.* I shut the door, walk out to a flower bed, lie down and sleep.

This one bothered me for years. Even though I still don't know what it means, after my vision in the hospital, I don't fear this dream. Or the one I had as a kid:

My mom had piled laundry piled on a chair in my room. Darth Vader sat in that pile of clothes. I cut off his head with a light saber. Lifting off Lord Vader's mask, I found my own face. That scared me then and for a long time.

Now I see I had been creating fears so that I could take the glory for defeating them. The whole time, I had been battling myself.

Before I fully understood this, my dreams after I defeated Darth Andy all contained some small ray of hope. I was beginning to feel confident that God was with me, even in my dreams. He always had been there. I was only just starting to see it, dream by dream.

Dark dreams haunt me every now and then. I'm able to turn them around now. In one recent dream, a man is holding a lantern to light my way. "If you don't want me here," he tells me, "I can leave."

I recognize Him as God and say, over and over, "I'm glad you're here. I'm sorry."

This time I could see that I wasn't apologizing for existing, for sitting on a swing, taking up space. I was letting God know I was sorry for not appreciating the light He gives in my dreams, and in my entire life.

This same new approach helps me make sense of things that would have troubled me in the past. A weatherman saying, "We'll have patchy drizzle tomorrow" might start me trying to picture what that would look like, how I would deal with it.

In the movie *Jurassic Park*, frog DNA gets patched to complete the creation of female dinosaurs. That DNA spontaneously turns some females into males. Soon, females get pregnant, eggs hatch, the population gets out of control. So many of these elements could have unnerved me.

Today, I insist on having a patchwork of any kind in my life. I refuse to force things along. I fill gaps where I find them. The fears I had been fighting, only to make them stronger, are no longer giants. Reality is a better place to live.

In the real world, tomorrow's forecast won't always be patchy drizzle, with a chance of dinosaurs.

The *Tao Te Ching*, Chapter 71: *Only when she is sick of her illness can she be healed.* I have experienced that. By fighting my fears and turning them into giants, I made that period of fear everyone goes through last far too long — about 20 years. With my fears fading, I am steering my ship toward wellness.

The less I am fake, the more my dreams improve. I can be one of the guests on *Nautilus*, smoking seaweed cigars with Captain Nemo, agreeing that they taste better than those made of tobacco. I know God will light the lanterns in the ship.

iving in an apartment in the city, people could watch me, see in through my windows. I might dance, then bow to the street. It was no different from a gerbil putting on a show in its cage, scooting through the tube, running on a hamster wheel — always putting on a performance, even when sleeping.

Privacy is one thing, but I felt the mirror intruding on my life, following me around. The public wasn't following me. I was. I had turned myself into Private Enemy #1.

Never truly alone, always being watched, I could never relax. When I stopped trying to be without myself, I could lose myself in God's love. That has made all the difference.

he night finally arrived. Like vinyl records melting in a car left out in the sun, I changed shape and walked out of a local bar forever. That place had been nicknamed "Vulture" because of the men who hung out there late at night. Trading vainglory for vulnerability, I headed home, feeling I was striding toward victory.

7

ALSO

IMMEASURABLE

I wouldn't change a thing. Going back to fix mistakes would be wasted time. God keeps preparing me for eternity, not this world. I remain imperfect. Storms still blow through. In a river raft, I can now enjoy it all, no longer trapped in a shark cage, my head always down.

One summer, at a camp for people with disabilities, I served as a counselor. The place wasn't run very well. Basically, I was assigned a group of clients and sent off into the woods. That was it. No planned activities. The woman who ran the place came to the counselor campsite to remind us, "You guys have to come up with activities to do on your own."

The camp had a pool. We were well fed at the cafeteria. But most days, we would just sit there. One counselor began to lose it. He felt he was wasting away. Like him, I wanted to be told what to do. All the boredom made me hate the place. Then I realized what had been eating me alive: freedom.

Terrifying, ungraspable at first, that freedom presented a real challenge. I didn't know how to use that gift yet. By the middle of summer, my group of clients and I were having a great time. So were the other counselors, many from the Czech Republic. They sang together in an outdoor amphitheater one evening. Their traditional Czech songs mixed with crickets chirping. Listening to that natural symphony, I could feel myself growing, maturing.

I encountered the same thing as a Job Coach. At first, not being instructed on what to do, I hated simply standing there. Then, in a pivotal moment, watching someone put security tags on liquor bottles, I noticed the creative names and pictures on the bottles.

I started imagining that I could pluck them with my fingers, pretending they made different sounds. In that sensory overload, I realized I was having fun. An employee at the store noticed it, too. "You're actually having fun," he told me. "Wish I had your job!"

I have never really lost that joy.

My responsibility as a Job Coach is to keep clients on track, to get them to focus on their work. I feel I also need to keep them full of joy and allow them to focus on their lives. A brief conversation about their upcoming weekend plans or how their relationships are going means so much to them. It gives them hope. And I get to have the time of my life.

Naturally, I overdid it. When I first started to be joy-filled, I played with my clients and we both got in trouble. Once, acting as if we were Teenage Mutant Ninja Turtles, my client ignored his job of cleaning and bussing tables. The boss busted us. From that day, I realized I could not be a distraction. Instead, I had to help the clients perform their jobs and enjoy their lives.

When I started working with one client, I'd take him to the beach. On the pier, he would see someone in an L.A. Lakers shirt and say, "Go Lakers." To a person wearing an SDSU t-shirt, he'd call out, "Go Aztecs." I felt ashamed—not of my client, but of my inability to control the direction of each interaction. I could have been back in a classroom as a Substitute Teacher, unable to control the kids. This client, however, opened me up to see a bigger picture.

In his acknowledgment of each person, he offered love in his hellos. He customized those loving hellos, based on whether they were a Dodger fan or rooted for the Chargers or wanted to save the environment. They were individuals to him. No matter what he said after that, the love still came through.

Everyone responded well to my client. I was the only one worrying. That helped me see how my own social skills had been keeping people at arm's length. I was learning that we are all connected by love. My client, by simply behaving in accordance with this principle, showed me that truth with each of his unique hellos:

"Go Andy."

Sometimes, my client would bring a football with him. He liked to motion to people on the pier or the beach to "Go long." He wouldn't actually throw the ball, he'd just keep walking. Once, however, he did let one go.

A group of teens – two boys and a girl – walked past with their heads down. My client motioned "Go long." I didn't pay much attention to what had become his predictable behavior. Then I saw the ball flying toward those teenagers. I saw blood, maybe a fight and more blood, police, hospital ER, stitches, law suit, pink slip.

At the last second, one of the boys snatched the football out of the air, directly in front of the girl's face. All three of the teens started laughing.

"This kind of stuff always happens to me!" the girl said.

The teen who caught the ball had his arms raised and did a victory dance, shouting, "That's why I'm on the football team!"

I felt like saying, "That kid can play for me." Then I realized, he was already on my team.

God used my clients to show me things. Each thing He revealed felt like the greatest thing ever. That's how God works. I could live an infinite number of lives and not be a step closer to fathoming how great God is.

God has shown me the need to be patient. This can be especially difficult. One of my clients likes to say, "I'm allergic to patience."

And I no longer say everything that pops into my head – the chief trait that had made me a numbskull.

Above all else, God has shown me to be open to love. I now spend each day with God doing His will and being close to some of my favorite people in the world. They renew my heart day by day. Love reigns in my life today.

I still panic. One client would call me on the phone, then hang up the moment his parents came back into the room, so sometimes I'd get cut off in mid-sentence. I worried this signaled something was wrong. It took a few times for me to realize that just making those phone calls was the point for him. He knew I would answer. He didn't need anything more than that. When it happens now, I can laugh and play my part in his game of reaching out for love.

The lesson of not saying everything that pops into my head applies to my writing as well. I once forced myself to write, getting way ahead of my thoughts. I became a numbskull on paper, too. Worse, I'd read my latest drafts at poetry readings, thinking I had to have something new each time. My attempt to be humble and honest kept backfiring. My unedited drafts weren't very good, and certainly not ready for prime time. Or late night.

Fortunately, God stepped in. If I owned a fruit stand, I wouldn't put out ripe fruit next to rotten fruit. I write fewer pieces now, waiting for God to move in me.

The writer who had felt he had to be a prophet, writing story after story to save the world with a philosophy no one had thought of before, got replaced by a more patient model. And patience can save the world, because it provides time and space for love.

Playgrounds at Drive-Ins had swing sets, where birds fluttered in the trees. Running to the concession stand, I would pass speakers on the driver's side windows of cars, each echoing off the other. Out of breath, I'd get a soda and some candy, feel the heat of the lights, the warmth leaking out from behind the counter.

My memories of Drive-Ins outnumber the few that still remain. An experience I had at a movie theater reminded me of watching that giant screen in the Drive-Ins, feeling part of the action. I went to see *The Poseidon Adventure*. At the moment in the film when the cruise ship capsizes and the lights on the ship flicker out, the theater flood lights came on. For a second, I actually believed I was underwater.

Art has the power to convince. TV ads try to do the same thing. As a Job Coach, I felt I needed to improve my brain function. So I considered taking *Prevagen*, an over-the-counter memory-enhancer made from jellyfish. *But jellyfish don't have brains*

My brother thought that eating raw jellyfish the same way Rocky Balboa ate raw eggs would work better than taking a *Prevagen* pill. I thought roasted jellyfish might taste better and imagined this scene:

"What's for dinner?"

"It's a surprise."

A giant tray cover is removed, revealing an 8-foot Man-of-War jellyfish – enough for the whole family! Memorable.

122

Whenever a *Code 100* blares over the loudspeaker at one grocery store, it serves as a Bat Signal for my client working there. He races into action, throws down a powder to absorb the liquid, then sweeps it all up.

He was with me at another store when we saw a shopper drop a jar of honey. Quick as a sprinter, my client dashed to the supply room, came back with absorbent powder and covered the honey and broken glass.

"That will only make it worse," the store manager told him.

Honey didn't absorb that powder and the powder couldn't absorb the honey. A supersaturated substance, honey attracts water. And it's the one organic compound that is virtually impossible to spoil. One report stated that it had been found on a 2000-year old Egyptian mummy. Though crystallized, the honey was still edible. There are chemical reasons for this – its high pH kills bacteria and bees process honey by means of an enzyme found in Penicillin A – but honey is the perfect food.

God's spirit has been the honey in my life. It doesn't go bad, never losing its power, so it can never fail me.

One client became my roommate. He had played football in high school, too. His summer two-a-day practices took place in Orange County, near the ocean. Mine were held in Upland, a foothill community near San Bernardino, where Stage 4 smog alerts and 100-degree temperatures were common.

Ironically, my roommate's football coach used to goad his players during Hell Week by asking them if they'd rather be in San Bernardino. And that same coach made his players pound their helmets and chant, "Foothill's coming, they want you, 1-2-3,1-2-3."

My football practices are just a blur now. I can only remember the facemask of my helmet and the sound of me running out of breath.

Many of my memories have compressed in that same way, with what appear to be meaningless details all that remains of them:

Safari Park Zoo – wild deer in the parking lot near the entrance. Mist making that image dreamlike.

123

Other memories contain more details. In these, I remember what I learned from those I had been hired to watch over.

Hundreds, maybe thousands, of crows would fly over my house each morning. A client believed that crows hung out by themselves during the day, then got together in the evening to party. Skeptical, he and I got in my car and followed a flock one evening, ending up at an elementary school playground. The field had turned black with crows.

Another client owned a walk-in aviary with more than 30 birds in it. An older man, he had grown up on an Oklahoma farm. He told stories as if pulling them from dreams. A character in all of these stories was The Chief. I came to realize this was God. Whenever a bird got out of the aviary, he would say, "That bird went to see The Chief."

He described a dream he had while wide awake: "The Chief's daughter has a horse for me. It's snow white." In a poem, I wrote that in his mind, *the mules are running free*.

He had found the freedom I was still searching for.

When I worked at a Senior Citizen's home, I became friends with a resident who suffered from Alzheimer's. Zella told stories in a Southern dialect. She talked about moving to Paris, where a house waited for her. When I showed her a map of Paris to find the location of the house, she laughed. "Not Paris, France. Perris, California."

She pronounced both cities the same way.

Listening to Zella as she sat in her wheelchair near the fireplace, I felt myself being tucked into a nook. Later, I would learn that a space on either side of a fireplace was called and *inglenook*. I wrote a poem that started, *Sitting in the inglenook, I thought about the flensing of whales.*

I dreamed about Zella's stories of her life on the farm, and felt privileged to hear them. I even began to feel sorry for others who walked by outside and couldn't listen in:

> Outside in the maze wind,
> a man with sunken knuckles bends
> to pick up flypaper.

Zella got to Perris, and that house was waiting for her.

124

At one poetry reading, I almost stood up and shouted, "This poem mentions blueberries. And blueberries have anti-oxidants. What if this offends someone who likes oxidants?"

One reason for that almost-outburst sprang from my feeling that I had been slandered over my own art, and the pain wouldn't leave me.

I blamed others for misreading my work. Then I blamed myself for a lack of clarity in my writing. The real reason became clear much later: Art is risk.

So is life. There are no guarantees.

A friend who loves going to Disneyland to make wishes at Snow White's Wishing Well taught me to pour everything into each wish. Making the wish, having the hope, that's what matters, regardless of the outcome.

One day, the mother of a client asked, "Is your Job Coach disabled?"

And, of course, I am. We all are.

The law might not consider me a person with disabilities. But I am. God knows I am. We all are.

None of us would say, "Don't breathe normally around that guy. He has asthma. You might offend him." And we wouldn't label him "Asthmatic Bob."

To make sure I wasn't talking about a homeless person, I wouldn't introduce a friend as, "This is Bob. He has a house."

Calling people disabled may be better than the old labels, but as long as labels are used, we're all lost. The moment I stopped categorizing people, I began to work well with my clients, all of whom are people with disabilities. Once I acknowledged we were the same, I no longer separated myself from them.

I no longer tell people, "I work with a group of disabled people. I'm their boss. They do good work." Today I say, "I'm a Job Coach. My clients do good work and succeed."

Once I might have been patronizing, treating my clients like children. I now open myself to their wisdom and friendship.

Three days a week I worked with Eddie. At 6'4" and 200 pounds, he was a fine athlete. In basketball, he could sink a 20-foot shot without effort. Looking at him, no one would think Eddie was autistic.

Whenever someone walked by him with a glass of water or soda, he would run after them, grab the liquid, pour it on his head, then rub some on his forehead, a little on his stomach and each of his legs. Those who knew him called it "the blessing."

One day, Eddie went to the beach with his class and he ran in the ocean. He kept going, as though he belonged in liquid.

Some called it suicide. I like to think Eddie eloped, mimmering at the horizon.

My client Deena used to make collages depicting how Disney characters related to the struggles in her life. Working on a new collage, she got on the *It's a Small World* ride. Suddenly, the image of Aladdin came to her mind, along with the movie's theme song, *A Whole New World*. At first, she thought God was sending a message that a man would come into her life and show her a new world. Then she began to wonder if the message meant she was in store for a ride of wonders.

She started work on a new collage. I agreed to take her to the *Disney on Ice Princess* show so she could catch the Aladdin performance. I ran into problems parking and had to use a gas station ATM, making us late. I started worrying we would miss the part of the show Deena needed to see. And it would be my fault.

My worry increased when, picking up the tickets at Will Call, I saw the long line to get into the arena. Finally inside, the whole place was dark. Suddenly, the lights came up and *A Whole New World* began playing. The Aladdin character skated out and took Jasmine off on a magic carpet.

Next to me at the railing, Deena was crying. I remember thinking, *God got us here at exactly right moment*. We stayed at the railing until Aladdin's number ended, then found our seats for the rest of the show.

Deena called a few weeks later to check in and tell me she would not be not be spending Thanksgiving with her family. She had decided to spend the holiday in her apartment, by herself. She told me should would set the table for two — one for her, one for God.

Not long after that, I received a call from my boss. Deena had been driving her scooter to work when she lost control, hit a car, then a pole. She had died.

The news shocked and saddened me. I gave those feelings to God:

> Her family was upset that she wasn't
> coming over for Thanksgiving.
> She said, "I will dine at my table.
> I will place two settings:
> one place will be for me
> one place will be empty.
> The empty place is for God."
> And it was as though God said,
> "I like your table,
> and your china is fine.
> But I've got a better idea.
> Let's eat at mine."

Tonight

Tonight I worked as a Job Coach in a Vons. The new grocery bagger I was coaching reminded me of someone who worked at the Vons that employed Deena.

All baggers had to tell checkers if they saw anything on the bottom of carts. The code word was *Bob*, for *Bottom of basket*. Deena's store manager liked to grind this in by asking, "Hey Deena, did you ask about Bob? How about that Bob?"

She had said her manager was relentless about it. I had joked that, for her manager's birthday, she should invite him to the movie, *What About Bob*.

I kept thinking about this tonight, chuckling to myself. Then I saw him. Checking out on my new bagger's line, movie star Richard Dreyfuss unloaded his items.

My client said, "I think he was in that movie. *What About Bob?*"

After carrying the groceries out to the actor's car, my client followed the rules and said he was not allowed to accept tips.

"In this economy?" Richard Dreyfus said.

When we got back inside and my client said, "He was a famous actor."

I said, "He's been in a lot of movies," I told him. "He starred in *Jaws*."

"No," my guy said. "He was in *What About Bob?*"

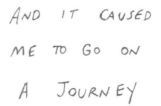

AND IT CAUSED ME TO GO ON A JOURNEY

n New Orleans for Jazz Fest, I lucked into getting the coolest cabbie in the world. "Look at that other cabbie in the fast lane," he said. "The slow lane is much faster on this stretch."

A few seconds later, the fast lane stopped and we cruised by. He found the best lane for each part of the drive, moving past all the traffic. On a Cool Cabbie high, I couldn't wait to get to my hotel room. I set my small bag on the bed, then I realized my suitcase was still in the cab. And the Cabbie was gone.

I called every taxi cab company in the phone book. I started with Yellow Cab, convinced the cab had been yellow. Next I called Checker Cab, thinking, "It could have been checkered."

Soon I heard myself emphatically telling one cab company, "It was a blue station wagon! I know it was."

Then: "It was a purple van! How many could there be?!"

I had no idea what the cab really looked like, but I was convinced. the coolest cabbie ever had to be pulling up to the hotel with my suitcase any time now. I walked outside to wait for him.

An hour later, I headed to my friend's condo. Keeping an eye out for my cab driver, I managed to get lost. Twice.

The next day, I spent the morning at Jazz Fest, then went to the Gospel Tent after lunch to meet my brother, who had just flown in. "I have your suitcase," he told me.

"I knew that cabbie was cool," I said. "I was telling everyone, watch, we'll hail a cab and it'll be him!"

My brother smiled. "He gave you his card. It was on the dresser when I got to our room."

When I caught my breath, I muttered, "But, if we did hail him, that would have been cool."

After the End

When my mom would drive us around, showing us things every time we got lost, we saw real life. I felt lucky to have my mom for a guide back then.

Since that time, I've come to see how blessed I have been to be so hopelessly lost that I could fully appreciate what it feels like to be so beautifully found.

God emptied me to fill me. My clients and friends taught me to love and be lovable.

My life has turned out to be more than I could have ever dreamed.

The journey continues.

Acknowledgements

Thanks to my family – my parents, brothers and sister, nieces and nephews, cousins, aunts and uncles – for putting up with me and helping me grow.

Special thanks to God, of course – always there for me, even when my foolishness was comical (or dangerous).

To my clients/angels – you called me at just the right time, inspiring me in momentous ways.

To friends, who put up with my tomfoolery and listened to my deep conversations that went nowhere, and to all the school districts and children, who taught me more than I taught them (which by now should be obvious.)

So many of my favorite authors – Lewis Carroll, L. Frank Baum, *The Simpson's* writers, George Orwell, *Parks and Recreation* writers, *Mother, Maiden, Crone* and countless others – for work used by God to inspire me.

And thanks to Bill Harding for being my editor and to Garden Oak Press for supporting a network of artists who can invest in and grow with our community.

Credits

Some poems and excerpts from poems in this memoir first appeared in the **San Diego Poetry Annual**.

Illustrations by the author

About the Author

ANDY PALASCIANO barely maintained a C+ average at four different state universities before finally graduating with a Bachelor's Degree in English from San Diego State (SDSU).

He immediately applied to be a substitute teacher.

He had to take two basic math classes, and pass a rudimentary math quiz before being given his Emergency Credential. The name of this credential itself, allowing him to substitute with no actual teacher training, should have told him something:

Emergency!

CPSIA information can be obtained
at www.ICGtesting.com
Printed in the USA
FFHW011250180419
51865936-57261FF